MUSIC TO MY EAR

MUSIC TO MY EAR

Reflections on Music and Digressions on Metaphysics

Michael Rubinstein

QUARTET BOOKS

LONDON MELBOURNE NEW YORK

First published by Quartet Books Limited 1985
A member of the Namara Group
27/29 Goodge Street, London W1P 1FD

British Library Cataloguing in Publication Data

Rubinstein, Michael
    Music to my ear.
    1. Music appreciation   2. Music — Psychology
    I. Title
    780'.1'5   MT6

ISBN 0-7043-2543-8

Phototypeset by AKM Associates (UK) Ltd,
Ajmal House, Hayes Road, Southall, London
Printed by Chanctonbury Press Ltd.
West Chiltington, Sussex

Contents

To Daniell Revenaugh but for whose blunt pencil my English would be even worse than my American . . . and I might never have come to tolerate Bruckner.

ACKNOWLEDGEMENTS

First to my family – Joy, my wife, and Imogen, Adam, Polly and Zac – for tolerating, usually, the sometimes almost intolerable; to Daniell Revenaugh, pianist and conductor, to whom this book is dedicated, for bringing me in with unerringly timed encouragement; to Jean Friend and then Anita Strickland for deciphering the often illegible; to Ann Comper for enabling me to discover the quality of Bartok's fifth string quartet, my gateway to New Music; to Anna Shuttleworth for her patient efforts to teach me to play the 'cello and to Ivan Aarons for his patience for rather longer, restraining my eagerness to play the violin even slightly out of tune; to Professor Robert Ornstein for indicating left hemisphere obscurities in and to Professor David Bohm for giving his blessing to the Postlude; to the Sufis who have striven to open my inner ear and to Robert D'Aubigny and Kim Coe for opening my eyes; and finally to Richard Baker who dispelled an author's last care – that it should not have been all a waste of time.

Acknowledgements are also due to: British Rail Funds Works of Art Collection; the Courtauld Institute of Art; Gerd Wolfgang-Essen; L'Hermitage, Leningrad; Maurithuis Museum, the Hague; Okresni Museum, Snemouni, Czechoslovakia; *Punch*; the Royal Academy; Sotheby's, London; the National Gallery, London; the Tate Gallery, London.

FOREWORD

Music in this country would never have survived without enlightened patrons. Michael Rubinstein is one of them, and he has decided to share with us in this book a lifetime of reflection on the art he loves and serves so well.

It is well known that Michael is by profession one of our leading solicitors. He is not one to seek the limelight, though he responds admirably when forced into it through being involved in some newsworthy case. Similarly he adopts a low profile in the world of music. There he is happy to operate behind the scenes, but his judgement and knowledge have brought him an influential role in a number of forward-looking musical enterprises.

He is a trustee of the Society for the Promotion of New Music and of the new Berlioz Edition, a director of Opera 80 and vice-chairman of the governors of the Purcell School. Like his great friend the late Sir Robert Mayer, he takes the uncompromising view that in musical education nothing but the best is good enough; and this applies to the creation of appreciative audiences as well as new performers. Hence Michael's long-standing membership of the board of 'Youth and Music', the organization created by Sir Robert to make fine music more readily available to young music-lovers. As a fellow-member of that board, I can testify to the value of Michael Rubinstein's wit and wisdom, sharpened by long experience of the law, in helping to overcome many a knotty problem.

In this book, too, Michael is very much concerned with the audience, with the quality of listening we bring to music. He clearly believes that every person present in a concert room contributes to the shared experience of live music; the listener no less than the musician is an integral part of the performance, and should be no less well prepared.

Excellence is the name of Michael Rubinstein's game, in music, law and life. Fortunately his tough intellectual standards are softened by a disarming modesty which makes the man a pleasure as well as a privilege to know, and the great appeal of this book is that he has put so much of himself into it.

Richard Baker, 1985

INTRODUCTION

On Gozo, a small island in the Mediterranean, I have often sat through long hot afternoons and evenings surrounded by the sounds of unsophisticated singing from the radio loudspeakers of local villagers. That music, slightly distanced from me but nevertheless intrusive has always seemed to suit the atmosphere there though I would not myself choose to listen to it. What would I choose to listen to on Gozo? *Flos Campi* by Vaughan Williams and Berlioz' *Nuits d'Été* headed a list I never tailed. But I was inspired by the question to examine my reasons for choosing to listen to one work rather than another at any particular time and place. My starting point would be my own experience and personal tastes.

As an addict of the gramophone, of fairly catholic classical taste sprinkled with bare patches, I regularly explore fringes of the recorded music catalogue. As an amateur violinist I am aware of the limitations of canned performances. Every performance that is not a re-creation is chronic, or clonic. Hence the temptation to acquire a number of different recorded performances of my favourite works.

A fascination of the Radio 3 *Record Review* programmes has been the reminder that the same work may be performed in a variety of different ways, in some cases on instruments with very different characteristics. A wide range of moods may be matched or induced: and may occasionally correspond with the intentions or aspirations of the composers themselves, for all we listeners or the performers know.

A musical diet of sunny symphonies of Haydn or of melancholy Shostakovich string quartets would soon induce a kind of indigestion. There is, anyway, a fabulous choice to avoid the risk of that and to match the mystery of moods and their impermanence.

Some may be relieved that this book is not a record guide listing and comparing works, performances and recording qualities to recommend some and to warn against others: that would too soon be out of date. Nor is the book a shrine to my subjective tastes and judgements. It should commend its readers to celebrate the wonder of human diversity.

Allowing for the variety and changeability of moods, I acknowledge that gaps in such a book are inevitable. The virtue and value of any book may not validly be measured in the printed words and sentences[1] which should, ideally, stimulate and feed the imagination like butterflies a buddleia. The thoughts so inspired may be noted down; and perhaps later discarded. But even unrecorded traces may fertilize and supply nourishment in other seed-beds of the mind.

Music is so pervasive in our civilization, so available, that it can barely be avoided yet it is largely ignored. An old friend of mine, a country clergyman, once told me that he thought one reason for today's almost empty churches may be that in former eras a church was the only place where people would expect inevitably to hear music performed, whereas nowadays . . . one reason for the almost empty churches: an excuse with an appoggiatura of truth?

Professional musicians among my friends regard my expressed love for music as suspect because I have music as a background to my work at home, where I must often read and write with a high degree of concentration. I dislike it as a background to conversation but prefer it to silence when I am working: provided, essentially, it is music which I want or am positively glad to hear. Not, definitely not, Glazunov or music for the guitar; classical jazz *in*, 'wallpaper' and pop *out* – my vaunted objectivity breached by persuasive subjectivity.

I have touched on mood, realizing that it may appear to explain the choice of a certain type of music, composer or artist, a particular work or performance. Alternatively mood *may* be invoked by music available by chance, for example at a concert or in a broadcast, and experienced initially in an unrelated emotional state.

Originally I intended to play a series of music menus for various occasions. First there was the hot Gozitan *à la carte* for which I have already suggested two items in the realm of 'balmy nacht-musik', not necessarily confined to nocturnal performance. Noting that sometimes moods change with the time of day, as with the seasons, I prepared for the *table d'hôte* programmatic works by Vivaldi, Sibelius, Ravel, de Falla, Stravinsky and other Western composers while not neglecting Indian ragas. Natural features – bare mountains, seas, heaths, hanging gardens, for example – would have added pieces by too many composers to be worth listing but certainly would include Mussorgsky, Debussy and Holst, and countless opera scenes according to their plots and settings.

In another realm is music to accompany specific activities – sea shanties, dance music, water music, firework music, music to seduce to, music while you work – if allowed and if it suits you *and* if you can't avoid it; but not for me *Music While You Work* – light music by the half hour, broadcast by the BBC during World War II to sustain the spirits of weary factory workers when air raids had disrupted much needed sleep; has any psychologist, I wonder, explained the success of this humane equivalent of whipping galley slaves.

Other categories were to include location music – for the open air, in salon or palm court for tea-time cakes and gossip; pervasive 'musak' in shops and (*pace* conscientious contributors to the *Good Food Guide*) in restaurants – without a vigorous and well-supported campaign we will have musak on public transport; also music to guide and accompany group activities – folk dancing, church services, football matches, films and broadcast series announced by signature tunes.

But when I came to write this book I found that I could not allow mere lists to provide its structure. Instead, my pen offered a sequence of no immediately obvious logic: a tour of ideas about listening to music which had evidently been accumulating among my scattered memories from early childhood. I found myself compelled at last to read a book whose spine had for years haunted me – the late Deryck Cooke's *The Language of Music*.[2]

Towards the end of his long final chapter, 'Large-Scale Functioning of Music Language', he wrote: 'Perhaps one day, after intensive research into the various aspects of the art – acoustical, physiological, psychological and simply musical – it may be possible, by correlating many findings, to discover *exactly* what it is that music expresses, and *exactly* how it expresses it; but if the attempt is made, it will have to be guided by the most meticulous regard for absolute truth, especially in the psychological field, where the final answer is likely to be found.' With most of that I agree: only I am wary of the use of words in any attempt to formulate 'absolute truth'.

It is no coincidence that my list of categories of music suited to different occasions is completely different from Deryck Cooke's list of 'various aspects of the art'. His study explores musical language as used consciously or sub-consciously by composers – he is interested in the 'original emotional impulse'. My starting point is that of the self-indulgent listener, and the ultimate emotional impact on him of what he chooses or happens to hear.

However, in lighting on the end of Deryck Cooke's monumental essay I found that I met him at the most sensitive point, where it matters. In his preface he wrote: '. . . one whole side of our culture is impoverished, since we deny ourselves the possibility of enlarging our understanding of human experience by a specifically musical view of it. After all if man is ever to fulfil the mission he undertook at the very start – when he first began to philosophize, as a Greek, and evolved the slogan "Know thyself" – he will have to understand his unconscious self; and the most articulate language of the unconscious is music.'

Whether music is indeed the *most* articulate language of the un-conscious I am not sure: poetry and painting and other art-forms are arguably no less articulate languages of the unconscious. Each of us has limited capacities for understanding. It is only through the particular 'windows' through which I view our culture and my individual place in it – unless and until I increase their number – that I can enlarge my under-standing of human experience: the principle is the same for everyone. If an appreciation of music is such a 'window' I would be foolish to do other than look through it with attention and wonderment.

Listening to music is generally considered passive, in contrast to the active, creative and re-creative practices of composing and performing. Nevertheless it may help man in an underlying mission to 'understand his unconscious self'. To a facet of that task – to 'Know thyself' – this book is devoted. Sometimes the thread of this theme surfaces to join explicitly the pattern of experiences described. Always it is there, harmonized no less when audible only to the inner ear.

---

1. cf. *The Book of the Book* by Idries Shah, Octagon Press, 1969.
2. OUP, 1959.

1
IN CONCERT

The Queen Elizabeth Hall was darkened, the platform as well as the auditorium, and hushed with unusual expectation – tension in anticipation of the unknown. It was in May 1968 and, with a brave friend who made no special claim to musicality but said, beforehand, he had an open mind, I was waiting for the start of an evening of improvised electronic music by AMM Music sponsored by an organization, Music Now, since, alas, defunct. An announcement was made: there would be no interval but we, the members of the audience, were invited to come and go as we pleased throughout the concert, for coffee, for exercise, even for escape. We took advantage of that suggestion later. But first we sat through an hour and more of music performed on a selection of instruments, including probably a guitar and a violin, a horn, a piano – I forget now precisely what. On the platform the performers wandered about in the near darkness, playing and adjusting equipment (so it seemed), while the music was amplified and electronically distorted or re-formed in various ways.

Often during that concert I was glad to be able to shut out the interminable simulated sound of goods trucks crashing into each other in a railway siding, spilling repeatedly, inexhaustibly, huge loads of resonant steel girders. All I had to do was to place my left hand over my left ear or plug my left ear-hole with a finger. Not even a lover of that '*Now* kind of *Music*' could have been offended by the sight of me,

thinking that if I couldn't stand the noise I should get out of the siding.
I left one ear uncovered throughout. Who could tell that I am
completely deaf in my right ear? (I cracked my skull in a motor-bike
crash when in the army in 1942.) So I sat through more of that concert
than my two-eared but plucky friend. And I really enjoyed the coda
lasting half an hour or so, a prolonged decrescendo . . .

In the 1920s my mother took me each year when I was old enough to
some of the Robert Mayer Children's Concerts in Central Hall,
Westminster. They were conducted by the ebullient Malcolm Sargent,
who bounced up and down at the piano to pick out tunes when
introducing the works to be performed, conveying his enthusiasm in a
hearty voice which echoed gorgeously round that acoustically im-
perfect hall. He was popular enough with me, however unpopular later
when he was less than affectionately known among orchestral
musicians, if not choirs, as 'Flash Harry'.

Those Children's Concerts were my earliest introduction to the
world of live orchestral music. Later I was lucky to attend many
concerts at the Queen's Hall, in the 1930s, and in the early months of
the war before it was bombed. There the acoustics were excellent. But I
mention the former because I remember vividly that I was often
inspired by the music (but do not now know *what* music) to allow my
imagination to fly me up from a seat in the circle and out over the stalls
and the orchestra itself. With what rapt attention should most children
who are not to become professional musicians be expected to follow
constantly the ebb and flow of musical form rather than to day-dream?
And not only children.

Honesty requires me to acknowledge that only at an organ recital in
a Paris church in 1938 and on a very few subsequent musical occasions
am I confident that my attention was held throughout. There was a
performance of Beethoven's 'harp' string quartet Op.74 by the
Guarneri Quartet in the Raphael Cartoon Room at the Victoria and
Albert Museum; on another memorable occasion the Hirsch Quartet
played the Ravel string quartet at a South Place Ethical Society Sunday
evening concert at Conway Hall. The first of these two may have been
an experience unique to me, the second seemed to be shared by the
whole audience.

Such experiences emphasize the inferior quality of one's listening
at other times. Many incalculable factors may be responsible.
The Guarneri Quartet were perhaps especially euphonious, playing

2

instruments made by members of the famous Guarneri family. The Hirsch Quartet was not generally regarded as of the first rank and I know nothing of its members' instruments. No one will ever discover the state of mind of the respective members of both quartets on those occasions which were so notable for me, nor will anyone recall the state of the weather which can so affect the quality of sound produced by strings, nor assess the quality of devotion, or whatever else matters, brought to the concerts by the two audiences. But even without histrionics, there being no 'flash' conductors to distract the mind through the eye, or 'great names to conjure with', some special, unusual feeling was imparted.

It occurred to me years ago, how curious is a public concert to which individuals travel from their various homes scattered throughout a city, squeezing through the doors and settling to relative tranquillity for a couple of hours (with a few short breaks for exercise and refreshment): and stimulated, sated and satisfied – or disgruntled – they pour out through the same doors and engage anew in their separate and apparently unconnected lives. And yet they came together, as it were by chance, to share a particular experience as 'an audience' – not just any random collection of people but people who deliberately yielded independence to become, in sum, *that* audience: and then drifted away from each other at the end of the concert so that *that* audience simply disappeared, disintegrated.

Such an audience is an entity whose elements want to share and, in the event, do share *something* of the same experience without any member necessarily being acquainted with any other before they assemble; or, beyond those contacts made, generally superficially, through the senses, seeking or getting to know any other before they disperse.

It is as if an audience meets to have something done to it by the performers (this concept applies no less, of course, to a theatre audience, and so on). Today there are commercial reasons why concerts are seldom given by professional musicians for one patron, just a small family group or a party of friends. And yet the very presence of an audience consisting largely of people who have come to hear a particular soloist or ensemble, or a particular work or programme, adds a dimension to the expectation of its members and

3

seems to wrest some extra quality from the performers. In this exchange it is as if a non-musical resonance is set up among all who are present.

No one performance listened to on the radio, still less on a recording however technically excellent, can provide the experience of a 'successful' public concert. The sharing of pleasure among people gathered together can apply as well round a gramophone as round a platform; but something else is required in the way of feedback to enable performers to transcend their customary excellence, at whatever level; or to attain a co-incident aim.

In early April 1977 the pianist Balint Vazsonyi performed the thirty-two piano sonatas of Beethoven, in chronological order and from memory, on the Saturday and Sunday of one weekend. In the programme notes he invited the members of the audience 'to participate in an unprecedented musical event', adding: 'It is my hope that at the end of the day you will feel elated by this unparalleled collection of masterpieces which represent the diary of a creative life. From the outset it has been my conviction that, together, we can create a musical experience that none of us could have under ordinary circumstances.'

After that weekend I saw notices in only two newspapers. In the *Sunday Times* (10 April 1977) Felix Aprahamian acknowledged that he had only sampled two of the morning sessions, and the performance of the three last sonatas on Sunday evening. He wrote: 'I think Mr Vazsonyi fairly made his point about "the greatest musical diary of all time", certainly with the faithful who followed him in the sequence of all thirty-two sonatas within two consecutive days. They undoubtedly entered into the spirit of the venture and rewarded him with a standing ovation at the end of Op.111 late on Sunday evening. But admiration for his musical integrity must be tempered by the fact that his performances varied widely in quality . . .'

In *The Times* (4 April 1977) Max Harrison wrote of the Saturday recitals only: 'Mr Vazsonyi believes, mistakenly in my opinion, that to hear these pieces, which span the composer's creative life, in such concentration is to learn something new about them . . . Yet the sheer quantity of music offered was such that the whole experience degenerated into a kind of test-to-destruction of pianist, listeners and sonatas. It need scarcely be added that Beethoven never intended his

4

music to be heard in this way, and as the long days [*sic*] wore on the impact of several great sonatas was considerably less than it ought to have been as one felt decreasingly able to make the active response which such works legitimately demand. Obviously Mr Vazsonyi's performance was a remarkable feat of memory and of carefully sustained energy, but it was hardly ever revealing musically. Of necessity these were utility readings, with the true weight of many subtleties of melody, rhythm, harmony and registration ignored.'

There followed in the same issue of *The Times* Joan Chissell's notice of the second day of the marathon: '. . .the strain of this ordeal showed so patently in wrong notes, unstable rhythm, memory lapses, blurred textures and disregard of finer dynamic gradation (far too much was too loud) that only intermittently could we glimpse what he was really trying to tell us about the sonatas as music. The final C major homecoming of Op.111 had long spells of memorable insight and authority. But a lifetime's work cannot comfortably be compressed into a weekend, and Mr Vazsonyi was neither fair to himself nor to Beethoven to attempt it.'

Were these critics really fair to Mr Vazsonyi? It was obvious that he was offering an exceptional opportunity to anyone who was prepared to embark on the marathon with him *and to remain with him throughout the whole of it.* We, 'the faithful' in Mr Aprahamian's phrase, had no right to expect better than 'utility readings'; if and whenever we felt that we were given better 'readings' than utility these must have been unexpected bonuses for us.

But such a legitimate concern with the 'readings' of individual sonatas or movements was, in my view, irrelevant to Mr Vazsonyi's announced purpose for those who elected to *participate* in the musical event: and the *event* was the whole marathon, from beginning to end. So much for these critics, doing 'their job' (and why *should* any of them have given up twenty-three hours over a single weekend to work?). Or nearly so much for them. I shall return in Chapter 2 to Mr Harrison's remark about Beethoven's intentions.

Meanwhile let me describe my own experience of the marathon. I followed it throughout from the score. As I do not play the piano (though as a child I learnt to play notes and boring old Czerny) I 'know' the sonatas as music heard and not as music played – a distinction which I regard as significant. My concern was not to see where Mr Vazsonyi slipped up (as must have been expected) but to enable me to maintain my concentration against the risks of distraction and fatigue. I can therefore confirm the validity of Joan Chissell's criticism of wrong notes, unstable rhythm, memory lapses, etc. But these intermittent imperfections were understandable *in the context of this marathon* and so 'forgivable': and did not matter because they did not detract from Mr Vazsonyi's purpose which we, the 'faithful' had deliberately set out to share with him.

Probably a 'greater' pianist could not and therefore would not have embarked on such an undertaking. Physically he or she might have accepted and discharged the challenge but psychologically it would have gone against the grain to give, inevitably, less than the best performance of any of the sonatas of which the artist would have been capable in the course of an ordinary recital of no more than three such major works. That is not to belittle Mr Vazsonyi's achievement, however, because his aim was to illuminate the inter-connectedness of and musical development through all the thirty-two sonatas, treated as a single manifestation of Beethoven's genius. To do this Mr Vazsonyi had to risk sacrificing his reputation; Joan Chissell for example had written: 'In the past I have usually been sufficiently stimulated by this pianist's lively musical intelligence, his sense of dedication too, not to be greatly disturbed by technical accidents.' But on this occasion, which Joan Chissell, in a passage I previously quoted, described as an 'ordeal', Mr Vazsonyi's musical intelligence and sense of dedication were directed precisely to the experience of a two-day marathon in which she had *not* participated. And in consequence she was bound to miss the point of the exercise.

I myself was overwhelmed by the complete experience. I was not alone in tears at the end. The standing ovation was spontaneous though earlier, during an interval, a poster was circulated among the 'faithful' so that we might sign it as a mark of our appreciation for Mr Vazsonyi's enterprise, stamina, musical integrity and courage which we evidently felt absolutely transcended the incidental shortcomings. We were not applauding the lapses, of course; nor were we in any sense applauding in spite of them. Could anyone who had not shared the first note and stayed the course understand that? And what had happened to Max Harrison's 'kind of test-to-destruction of pianist, listeners and sonatas'?

An inability to maintain rapt attention throughout a concert, or a single work however brief, or even one movement, is evidently universal and almost invariable. That does not, apparently, deter people from going to concerts. Might it not then be one of the attractions?

I have already described an early predilection on my part for day-dreaming. But that is only one of the many forms of distraction enjoyed or endured by concert-goers. Everyone who is not actually engaged in transcendental meditation, or something very like it, hardly ceases to fidget for a moment, mostly quite unconsciously. The need to fidget is epitomized by the incessant beating of near-time by the intrusive conductor-manqué who knows no better. What was going on in the minds of other members of the audience at a concert in the Queen's Hall when I could not take my eyes off the Prince of Wales (later, briefly, uncrowned King Edward VIII), sitting in the circle with his brother Prince George, who imitated, obviously in a state of semi-inebriation, every gesture of Sir Thomas Beecham? Of course everyone's hearing was frozen at the sight of this mildly sensational activity.

At another Beecham concert there were two empty seats in front of me during the first item, an overture no doubt. Before the commencement of the next work, a symphony or concerto, Sir Thomas turned and faced the audience with his arms crossed, silent. Two latecomers crept along the row to occupy the empty seats, under his severe gaze every inch of the way. Self-consciously they subsided, relieved that their ordeal was, as they assumed, at an end. Not a bit of it. 'Madam, do not smoke!' rapped Sir Thomas, then turned through a hundred and eighty degrees; and the music commenced. The miserable offender in front of me promptly stubbed out her cigarette (I know not on what) and burst into tears, to sob visibly and audibly throughout the whole of the first movement; then, with her equally miserable friend, she stumbled out before the second. No wonder I can recall nothing of the music.

Even without a Tommy Beecham or a Toscanini, with or without gimmicks, to electrify the atmosphere, there is an element of adventure in concert-going which may be part of the attraction. It is a little like attendance at a motor-cycle track where after several races one of the *aficionados* was heard to say anxiously to his companion, 'Can't understand it; still there's bound to be a nasty tumble soon.' At a concert there is the risk of a fluffed entry or simply a catastrophic enforced break in continuity. For instance I recall the soloist in a violin concerto who, when a string broke, exchanged his fiddle immediately for that of the leader, who equally promptly swapped it for that of his colleague at the first desk. The soloist carried on so fluently that a member of the audience listening with closed eyes might have noticed nothing untoward.

In contrast I remember a concert (I think it was at the Albert Hall) when a string broke with a loud jangle in the concert grand played by Rudolf Serkin in a concerto. The conductor lowered his baton and the orchestra petered out randomly. Rudolf Serkin ran round and with a bare hand (what else?) tore the offending wire from its tangling with those which remained secure, ran back and sat on his stool, poised. 'G' said he or the conductor – or it may have been 'H' – and away they went as if never halted for a moment. But *his hand!* I thought throughout the remainder of the concert; and I still do.

More recently the Aeolian String Quartet were giving a recital, in aid of the Purcell School for musically talented children, attended by many of its pupils. Someone suffered a broken string. They stopped at once while the player most efficiently changed it. The leader, Emanuel Hurwitz, as he raised the neck of his fiddle to resume, turned to the audience and with a disarming smile said, 'And then . . .'. What a lesson in composure!

Too frequently concerts are punctuated if not interrupted by coughs and sneezes; and even by whispering among the inexperienced and the inconsiderate. These are hazards to which concert-goers submit voluntarily. At one time or another each of us has probably offended. Only one's own unhappy lapses – as when a failure to swallow allows a drop of saliva to erupt in the windpipe – enable one to bless the grace of God at the occurrence of a like explosion in someone else's autonomic system.

Less forgivable are the programme-flutterers; and those who suffer from premature exultation, consistently applauding while the sound of music, to say nothing of its elevating impact, abides.

But – and this but is my true target – what are such external distractions beside the almost ceaseless chattering and chirping within? Does it help concentration to read programme notes during instead of before and after the performance of the work to which they refer? Does it help concentration to watch the conductor's gestures or the musicians' voluntary and involuntary movements and grimaces? Yet how many listen always and only with the eyes closed during concert performances or follow the score so that the eyes may reinforce, if they do not contradict, the evidence of the ears?

These are not rhetorical questions. They are radical: they go to the root of concert-going as a lifestyle. We imagine or pretend that the inherent, as distinct from the incidental, distractions help us to 'enjoy' the music: perhaps they really do. Or do we mean that they are part of the pleasure-process we expect or hope to enter into when we go to a concert? If so it is really the distractions which attract us rather than the music!

Put more crudely, the music is only one of the distractions, not necessarily the most important, which draw us to a concert. Other distractions may include company, for the gregarious; and sex, or at least an interchange with some underlying, hidden, perhaps repressed sexual content or connotation which is at once delightful and hypnotizing, sometimes sliding into ennui or disaster.

But don't be put off concert-going . . .

2

A COMPOSER'S INTENTIONS,
A LISTENER'S MOOD

It would be foolish to be put off persevering with a musical work just because, on the first hearing, it seemed unattractive, or worse than that.

Of his harsh fourth symphony Vaughan Williams is quoted as saying 'I don't know whether I like it, but it's what I meant.'[1] Such a remark refers to the language of music, what the composer intended to imply: but not necessarily to what any listener infers. So a poet conveys meaning within the lines and verses, between the words, beyond the context. Each reader of or listener to a poem, each listener to a musical work, will get a unique message – or invent one of his own.

In his *Times* notice of the first day of Mr Vazsonyi's marathon Max Harrison wrote somewhat snootily: 'Beethoven never intended his music to be heard in this way': nor, one may suppose, his *Hammerklavier* sonata Op.106 to be heard as an accompaniment to a ballet, or broadcast or taped. Already we glimpse all those inescapable arguments about authentic instruments and style which are healthy manifestations of the rightful concerns of musicians and musicologists. A composer's intentions as evinced in his scores may be respected in his lifetime and protected by copyright; subject to that legal protection his compositions belong to mankind to use, to misuse, to enhance, to exploit. If he performed or conducted any of his works on record – once only – it may be supposed that all may know what he wanted to represent as authentic. But, like those who will perform or conduct the same works afterwards, the composer himself was only human, may have lacked ideal skill or recorded in less than ideal physical or environmental conditions. Others should feel free to aim to produce sounds which feel right for them.

Should keyboard music written before the piano was invented be played on a piano? I do not object to 'authentic type' (as distinct from 'authentic-to-a-certain-degree') music-making provided that it enhances my appreciation of the music itself. Gimmickry I abhor. But music composed for the harpsichord can sound splendid, though in a different way, on a piano – but not, alas, when performed by Glenn Gould, for he upsets the balance by omitting all repeats; no piano performance is likely, however, for my pleasure, to replace Mme Landowska's harpsichord version of Bach's forty-eight preludes and fugues – 'version' naturally for that harpsichordist is recorded playing on the modern instrument, a Pleyel, with an idiosyncratic choice of registrations and her magnificently flamboyant style.

Throughout his '48', also known as *The Well-Tempered Clavier* (i.e. the clavichord tuned to equal semi-tones), Bach left no directions as to how he intended them to be performed. In her Prefatory Notes to the recording made in 1949 and issued on LP in 1971 Mme Landowska made a number of bold statements from which I quote a few:

> *The Well-Tempered Clavier*, rich, colorful, and ever changing, with the broad polyphony of its fugues arranged in choirs – how could it be confined to the limited domain of the clavichord when Bach had a harpsichord at his disposal? . . . All these preludes and fugues are simply inconceivable on the timid clavichord.

> Were the preludes composed with the intention of coupling them with the fugues of the same tonality or as independent pieces? Bach's biographers have busied themselves with this without reaching a conclusion one way or another. Even admitting that these pieces may have been composed separately at different periods during his life, it is plain that Bach selected and coupled them on account of a very subtle affinity which might escape those who look for a literal resemblance.

We do not know if it was Bach's wish that the forty-eight preludes and fugues be performed in their entirety in the same order in which he bestowed them on us.

Deryck Cooke, after discussing listeners' emotional reactions to the 'essentially painful connotation' of a minor chord with the fifth uppermost which he describes as obvious in all of a number of different examples which he specifies, adds:

> Of course, to a more subtle degree, a piece of music does convey something different to each normally responsive listener. Here is how Aaron Copland puts it: 'Listen . . . to the forty-eight fugue themes of Bach's *Well-Tempered Clavichord*. Listen to each theme, one after another. You will soon realize that each theme mirrors a different world of feeling. You will also soon realize that the more beautiful a theme seems to you the harder it is to find any word that will describe it to your complete satisfaction. Yes, you will certainly know whether it is a gay theme or a sad one . . . Now study the sad one a little closer. Try to pin down the exact quality of its sadness. Is it pessimistically or resignedly sad; is it fatefully sad or smilingly sad? Let us suppose that you are fortunate and can describe to your own satisfaction in so many words the exact meaning of your chosen theme. There is still no guarantee that anyone else will be satisfied. Nor need they be. The important thing is that each one feels for himself the specific expressive quality of a theme, or, similarly, of an entire piece of music. And if it is a great work of art, don't expect it to mean exactly the same thing to you each time you return to it.'[2]

From the above I would expect any open-minded reader to be satisfied that Mr Vazsonyi's marathon was wholly justified in conception, for musical and non-musical reasons, irrespective of Beethoven's 'intentions' for the performance of the complete canon of his piano sonatas.

There is of course no reason why the ambitious discophile should not play all those sonatas, in the order of composition, with any single pianist's set of recordings – and, given the stamina, within a period of twenty-four hours instead of Mr Vazsonyi's thirty-eight. But the experience would be bound to fall short of what Mr Vazsonyi offered. The recordings would have been made under studio conditions over a far longer period and in an order resolved for reasons of commercial expedience and practical convenience. The recorded pianist would not have embarked on the recording sessions with Mr Vazsonyi's aims or his research and reflection to underpin them. And, above all, the 'forcing-house' environment – for performer *and* audience – essential to Mr Vazsonyi's purpose, would have been absent. There would be no lapses, but also no magic because the recordings were not made on an 'occasion', in the context of a particular project essentially shared by all those participating throughout.

Mr Vazsonyi's note on Beethoven's final piano sonata Op.111 reads:

There seems little doubt that this last sonata is his autobiography: catastrophe and elevation. The tragedy which struck him down we meet in the *Maestoso*; his struggle and will to survive is portrayed in the *Allegro*; the peace he found is in the sublime *Arietta* – again a vocal title, but no longer resembling the human speech. It is quite beyond anything in the human vocabulary and its own metamorphosis takes it full circle. If one needs more proof, the entire sonata in C minor (Beethoven's most personal key) teems with references to countless preceding works: Opus 13, Opus 31 No.1, Opus 31 No.2, Opus 53 – to mention but a few. When it finally reaches the stars, the last question is asked and the reply is not only the inversion of the *Arietta*'s head-motive, but in fact the same two notes with which the entire journey began way back in 1795, in the first sonata in F minor. Coincidence? I invite you to decide.

To return to the matter of a composer's intentions, or the lack of them, in relation to the *use* made of his work is to open on to a most sensitive subject. It should not on that account be ignored, of course. We may admire the sheer professionalism and musicianship of the Swingles and yet deplore their impertinence so to maltreat Bach's works as-the-composer-cannot-have-intended: still, the music they make is *enjoyable*, even 'exciting' (at least when heard for the first time).

What then about *Bach Goes to Town*? We can forgive George Rochberg for such borrowings as in his *Ricordanza*, soliloquy for piano and cello (1972), a commentary on the opening solo cello statement of Beethoven's C major sonata Op.102 No.1 – after all Beethoven himself wrote sets of variations for cello and piano, and for other combinations of instruments, on themes of Mozart and others. Would he have complained of the swinging of his fifth symphony in Walter Murphy's *A Fifth of Beethoven* (from the film *Saturday Night Fever*) or in *Roll Over Beethoven* by Electric Light Orchestra (provided his copyright were duly protected, of course)?

Innumerable musical compositions of impeccable repute quote phrases from other composers' works. Bach and Handel, among many, have quoted from their own works and even used whole movements more than once. But genius can transform a trifle into a masterpiece (e.g. Beethoven's *Diabelli* variations) and will not *depend* on the work of others for inspiration let alone for padding.

My concern is to discriminate between vitalizing and trivializing arrangements. I am bound to confess that pragmatism dictates my attitude – what cannot be prevented should not be dubbed a crime. The laws governing copyright and performing rights are complicated enough without the extra burden of regulating my efforts to whistle well-known tunes correctly or my reckless indifference as to whether I succeed.

When the BBC initiated the Third Programme, which later became Radio 3, its elitism was attacked by philistine journalists. I remember an *Evening Standard* leading article, written, I assume, at the instigation of its then proprietor, Lord Beaverbrook, which raised my blood pressure. I was tempted to waste my time writing to the editor to explain why the then most low-brow broadcasting station should be sacrificed instead, until it struck me that to threaten to deny their favoured programmes to the (relatively) uncultured majority would deservedly and assuredly speed the demise of the Third Programme. Only by graciously encouraging the availability of choice for a variety of tastes, measuring the widest practicable gamut of brow levels, could I expect my minority predilections to be catered for regularly. Fortunately, someone in a position to control these things at the BBC evidently shared my vision. Later the newspaper mellowed – or came under more mature control.

The point is that I do not believe that the 'bad' will drive out the 'good' providing that the 'good' is readily enough available and the opportunity exists and is taken freely to make public comparisons. Hence my belief in the inestimable value of music clubs, gramophone recitals and music discussion groups, not patronizingly to provide 'enlightenment' but to extend horizons of understanding, even sometimes 'technical' understanding, and appreciation. And every encouragement should be given, including subsidies to concert- and opera-going to which, ideally, radio and record listening would be supplementary. Which brings us back to the all-important question of the attention with which we may grace any opportunity to listen to music.

What of Aaron Copland's recommendation that one should study a sad theme a little closer (than on first impression, presumably)? He advocates trying to 'pin down the exact quality of its sadness' to question whether it is pessimistically, resignedly, fatefully or smilingly sad. Or, I would add, pseudo sad, perhaps not really sad at all?

That could be an interesting exercise for some, involving the use of words chosen as accurately as possible to describe nuances of one's subjective feelings on the occasion. It was perhaps central to the concern of Deryck Cooke who quoted it in the context of his investigation of 'the language of music'. But for my purposes it seems rather artificial; and anyway does not accord with my chosen perspective.

My interest is to discover how in practice I respond to 'sad' and other music, not as an incident in an academic exercise but in the course of my listening life. I am not a manic-depressive but I recognize ripples, if not waves, curving on either side of a norm of relative tranquillity. I do not regard myself as a hedonist: in general terms I believe – or at least imagine – that I live for understanding rather than for pleasure. Should I not then, logically, deliberately avoid listening to 'sad' music – irrespective of the refinements of categories of sadness?

To pursue the implications of Aaron Copland's analytical method, I should ask what if I *were* a severe manic-depressive? Would I seek out 'sad' music to listen to when I was already depressed or try to listen only to 'happy' music at those times in the hope that I would be helped by it to swing into a more agreeable or supposedly desirable, manic, state? If, in reality, either end of that scale is, to say the least of it, anathema for the victim and those involved with him, he needs something stronger or subtler than – and different from – sense impressions to reduce markedly the extremes over which he has no control. Music, 'sad' or 'happy', would therefore be irrelevant to his chronic dis-ease.

My choice, if I make it, of 'sad' rather than 'happy' or 'neutral' music to listen to on any occasion is not, so far as I have noticed, a direct response to a mood which I would categorize as 'sad', or 'happy', in order to prolong it or to be wooed or shocked out of it. Nor does 'sad' music, for example, make me sad or, as the case might be, more sad; or help me to become happy. In terms of Deryck Cooke's language of music, a work may be saying 'this is sad music', but it does not say to me 'this is music to make you sad'. If it said any such thing then would not I and many others be tempted to reply 'Why should I want to be made sad', or to have my sadness increased or prolonged? That would invite the answer 'Of course you shouldn't!'

Nevertheless I have to acknowledge that I find music suitable to some moods which may *in general* be designated 'sad'. I am trying to distinguish such moods from the occasions for which it is customary to regard 'sad' music as appropriate – notably the death of someone with whom one has been at least amicably associated or for whom or for whose grieving relatives and close friends one has respect. The distinction is important because grief on the death of a loved one can turn quickly to self-pity – a very different emotion. The occasion of mourning for a public figure is traditionally accompanied by funeral marches, dirges and other 'sad' music and for this reason is now associated, I suspect for many people, with a mere semblance of grief; or it may serve to induce a real feeling of grief. How often and for how many of a mass of 'public' mourners does such music reflect sincere feelings?

Let not the suitability of any particular kind of music for particular occasions be taken for granted merely because it is traditional. 'Here comes the bride! Here comes the bride!' is the moment for which we have been waiting in church, translated, its vulgarity enhanced on the organ, from the chorus accompanying the couple into the bridal chamber in the third act of *Lohengrin*. This music gives me a message which sounds like 'She got her man! She got her man!' rather than 'There goes the bride.' A white wedding is naturally a joyful occasion, but the sense of triumph and possessiveness smacks of hubris. I await the statistics to prove that significantly more marriages than average accompained by this hearty hymn end in divorce. (Of course 'She got her man!' is a shameful reflection of the male chauvinistic myth that women chase into the marriage compound their natural prey, reluctant, freedom-loving men.)

Mendelssohn's Wedding March from his incidental music for

Midsummer Night's Dream conveys to the sensitive listener an altogether different atmosphere. The trace of triumph is lightened by a jauntiness which yet avoids the optimism of 'they'll live happily ever afterwards'. It says, to me, rather 'whatever the future holds let us at least enjoy this wedding now: anyway it's one imaginary person marrying another – you see!' That is surely just what Mendelssohn must have intended, to accompany the fairy wedding in Shakespeare's play.

I have pondered what other piece of music might be suitable for the occasion of a wedding, at the same time avoiding the solemnity and that fearsome hubris. I admire more than any other work by Stravinsky (though he is not one of my favourite twentieth-century composers) his exotic ballet-oratorio *Les Noces*, but it is a little long for an interlude in the formal ceremony. *Greensleeves* conveys tenderness 'in sickness and in health' (even in Busoni's intermezzo in his opera *Turandot* – he knew better, though, than to suppose it was a Chinese tune), but for many that would not be quite the right note to strike. 'Our tune', particularly, should not be open to selection otherwise than by the affianced couple however distracted they may be, at the time when the arrangements are being made, by more mundane deliberations.

The traditional solution is a convenient one on 'public' occasions for several reasons: on the last night of the Proms, for example, appropriate emotions are aroused by the expected rendering of *Rule Britannia*. The alternatives are virtually infinite and would have to be monitored in most cases by people who are not sufficiently interested or knowledgeable to make a meaningful choice and who could not be sensitive to such nuances as I have touched upon in the footsteps of Aaron Copland and Deryck Cooke. Further, individual choices, however 'sincere', might give offence to some who would be listening – not everyone would appreciate *Colonel Bogey* at a funeral – and might present practical problems for performance.

A sensitivity to non-verbal nuances may only be acquired by much exposure to nuances which are not, at once, recognized as such. A clever manipulator, like a wise counsellor, may inspire a response where there was none before, or where formerly it was weak or unfocused. Such a use is characteristic of much film music.

What seems to me important is to avoid an attitude of not *caring* what is to be performed or played.

I am specifically distinguishing an attitude of not caring whether anything is to be performed from one of wanting something to be performed but not caring what it is or how it is played. Significantly, attitudes, acquired from earliest childhood and every subsequent environment and superimposed upon genetic and possibly zodiacal characteristics, delineate all our relationships, with others and of course, though seldom acknowledged, with ourselves.

---

[1] In *An Encyclopaedia of Quotations about Music* (compiled and edited by Nat Shapiro, David & Charles, 1978, p.64) the remark is wrongly referred to Vaughan Williams' *London* symphony, as attributed to Sir Adrian Boult in a broadcast on 1 August 1965.

[2] Aaron Copland, 'What to Listen For in Music', quoted from *The Language of Music* op.cit.

3
ALONENESS AND IDENTITY

All my adult life I have avoided a long look at that question, most fascinating for anyone, 'Who am I?' Just as I take seriously the risk to the eyes of more than a flashing glance at the sun, I sense a danger in more than a moment's contemplation at a time of this enigma, my Self. So whom do I fool when I avoid a long look at a stunningly attractive woman?

From early childhood I learnt to associate my identity with my name. 'In the army you're only a number' I was told years later, on joining the Territorials in 1939. I didn't believe it: a number was merely a convenience for the authorities, fitting a common pattern, avoiding eccentricities and all risk of duplication. But no soldier, so far as I know, was ever at risk of mistaking his number for himself. If there were an error in one digit on any occasion it had to be corrected for the sake of good order and the avoidance of confusion. Spell my name Rubenstein, however, instead of Rubinstein and I felt – and feel no less today – disorientated and affronted.

Two closely connected experiences engendered by the non-recognition by others of one's identity, which render urban life disagreeable or worse to millions of citizens in our culture, are the feelings of isolation and insecurity.

Curiously the cure for a sense of being alone (not by any means necessarily the same as feeling lonely) is not company: that, in the ordinary way, would terminate being alone. One may *feel* alone in company – sometimes more alone than when by oneself. So to *be* is one thing and to *feel* is something quite different: both meaningful in their contexts.

When first produced in London at the Arts Theatre in 1953, Samuel Beckett's *Waiting for Godot* was regarded by many as a deeply pessimistic play. Two tramps occupy the stage, passing the time in inconsequential chatter while they wait – wait for whom they know not; there is an interruption in each act by two men on a journey linked by the lead by which one, a mentally seared tyrant, secures the other his mentally retarded slave to his will – until their roles are dramatically reversed. A fifth character, a small boy, brings a message from time to time from 'Godot' to say that he is delayed. The change in the tyrant–slave relationship was for me especially illuminating. And the fact that the boy came from 'someone' was a message of hope, ground for confidence, a deal sounder than optimism. I recall the sprayed graffito on London street walls in 1979, '99% is shit'. Fantastic! Some vandal actually has faith that as much as one per cent is *not* shit!

So, Beckett says, we are not 'alone' in our ones and twos and threes, in spite of appearances and experiences which suggest isolation. How can we decorate our lives with indestructable reassurance? The mystic has found one way but mysticism is for that (non-mathematically, non-statistically calculated) one per cent. The rest of us search for re-assurance and re-re-assurance through reminders. For some people a nightly trip round the public house helps, for others recourse is had to subtler or more desperate subterfuges, the peep round the lace curtains; the loiter at the street corner; the radio or television left on permanently; the telephone. The solitary tippler, the compulsive sucker of sweets or the chain-smoker seem to be seeking a nipple substitute or compensation for a lack of nourishing companionship.

Certainly listening and half-listening to music can equally serve as a substitute for a satisfying relationship or at least agreeable company. But it would be silly to suggest that the choice of one work rather than another represents a choice to represent the company one misses or would wish present. The choice of 'Nimrod' from Elgar's *Enigma* variations for funerals and memorial services is significant. Elgar's own notes describe the variation bearing this name as the record of a long summer evening talk with A. J. Jaeger who 'discoursed eloquently on the slow movements of Beethoven, and said that no one could approach Beethoven at his best in this field, a view with which I cordially concurred'. But he mentioned that 'Something ardent and mercurial in addition to the slow movement would have been needful to portray the character and temperament' of his friend. He also observed that 'The variations are not all "portraits"; some represent only a mood, while others recall an incident known only to two persons.' The opening bars of the 'Nimrod' variation were 'made to suggest' the slow movement of Beethoven's Opus 13 piano sonata, *The Pathétique*. Nothing mournful, nothing obviously suitable for condolence. No self-pity, no sentiment of mass grieving. Just a recollection of rare fellowship that, portrayed with Elgar's sensitivity and patent sincerity, is more surely consoling than any evocation of private or public woe.

With benefit of Elgar's own commentary, the distinction in this instance is clear between the composer's 'intentions' and the listeners' impressions. It matters not whether Elgar intended in 'Nimrod' to present a partial musical portrait of A. J. Jaeger, or to represent in musical terms a mood which a memory of his friend evoked or to recall the incident of a particular conversation between them on the subject of Beethoven's slow movements. This variation has, in practice, seemed fitting to console mourners. It can seldom portray even approximately a remembered quality or characteristic of the individual mourned. It may convey rather a sense of steadfast friendship of universal application – universal, that is, within a restricted 'universe' corresponding to such music as Elgar's in socio-anthropological terms.

For our British culture and our time Elgar's music, when not pompous and circumstantial, can set up a resonance of mood, like Bach's, which is not ephemeral. But Elgar is not, of course, unique in this.

When Parry's setting of Blake's poem 'Jerusalem' ('The New Jerusalem' from his *Milton*) is sung each week at meetings of The Women's Institute and each year at the last night of the Proms it gives an exceptional pleasure to every participant who is not tone-deaf. The words alone express idealism buried in everyone's heart from the days of late adolescence. Worldliness, perhaps sophistication, may overlay this idealism with cynicism but, magically, Blake–Parry break through, every time. Dire experience and customary hypocrisy seem unable to withstand the assault of this particular example of optimism combined with enthusiasm, aspirations to sing about even – or especially – when the ship is sinking. The members of The Women's Institute sing in a community discomforted by the frustrations of an increasingly discredited Welfare State and evidence that the institution of conventional marriage is losing ground to a new balance of relationships between men and women; do they nevertheless aspire together – but apart from their menfolk, fathers, husbands, lovers, sons – to build 'Jerusalem in England's green and pleasant Land'? Still 'Among these dark Satanic Mills'? The Prom audience is letting off steam. It is not only the euphoric words of the poem or its sentiment which epitomize the climax of the season or the rousing tune but rather a heartfelt combination of both.

Afterwards, and for most of the time, everyone who has just joined in singing 'Jerusalem' ceases from 'Mental Fight' and his/her (metaphorical) Sword sleeps in his/her hand. As Blake put it in his brief poem *Eternity* 'He who binds himself to joy Does the winged life destroy; But he who kisses the joy as it flies Lives in eternity's sun-rise.' That is, I am sure, partly the spirit in which people come to listen to music otherwise than as background sound. To become a slave to joy is to destroy its life – its life-enhancing possibilities. To be obsessed with an ideal or a moral principle is no less likely to destroy its point, its virtue, its credibility.

So let us kiss music, a joy, as it flies. Instinctively we realize the senselessness of trying to nail it to any certain or final 'meaning' however simple or subtle. Music's influence on us, and on those joys we seek to invoke, lies in its power to remind us of all sorts of things!

A piece of music will remind us of itself if we have heard it before. It may also remind us of other music, not necessarily by the same composer: but this is to assume both some familiarity with the relevant stream of music and the knack of remembering sounds not always recognizable as tunes. We may be reminded of a place where the work was first heard, or heard in memorable circumstances; or of the company present when we heard it in an emotionally affecting situation. And above all it reminds us subliminally of our moods and their changes which we find interesting, pleasurable, and possibly inspiring to recall.

In a short piece, music may encapsulate a stable mood. But an overture or a prelude (to anything or nothing) may well present us with variety within its compass. We expect a longer work to cover a range of changing moods, contrasts and challenges culminating, generally, in final resolution.

In his piano sonatas, about sixty in all, Haydn kept loyally to a fairly standard formula, and produced a stream of fascinating ideas as original and stimulating within sonata form as Domenico Scarlatti in over 550 so-called sonatas for harpsichord, each an exciting germ, hardly developed at all. To fall into what Donald Tovey[1] called 'the common errors of a bird's eye view of music', distanced as I am by relative ignorance, it seems to me that Beethoven added a new dimension to the form, apparent notably in his last sonatas from Op.101 onwards, by an extended use of swift changes or alterations of mood. But that's how we are! 'Beethoven's psychology . . . is always right. His music is, in fact, a supremely masterful and hopeful criticism of life.' (Donald Tovey, *Beethoven*, op.cit. p.2.)

Compare this passage from a novel:

Some things can't be ravished. You can't ravish a tin of sardines. And so many women are like that; and men. But the earth . . .!

The rain was abating. It was hardly making darkness among the oaks any more. Connie wanted to go; yet she sat on. But she was getting cold; yet the overwhelming inertia of her inner resentment kept her there as if paralysed.

Ravished! How ravished one could be without ever being touched. Ravished by dead words become obscene, and dead ideas become obsessions.[2]

Not untypical Lawrence, but I prefer the relative classicism, based on a firmer framework of truth to life, of Beethoven. Or James Joyce: 'Touch me. Soft eyes. Soft soft soft hand. I am lonely here. O, touch me soon, now. What is that word known to all men? I am quiet here alone. Sad too. Touch, touch me' (Stephen Dedalus on Sandymount strand).[3] And Molly Bloom, in spate:

. . . your blouse is open too low she says to me the pan calling the kettle blackbottom and I had to tell her not to cock her legs up like that on show on the windowsill before all the people passing they all look at her like me when I was her age of course any old rag looks well on you then a great touchmenot too in her own way at the Only Way in the Theatre royal take your foot away out of that I hate people touching me afraid of her life Id crush her skirt with the pleats a lot of that touching must go on in theatres in the crush in the dark theyre always trying to wiggle up to you . . ., *etc.*[4]

For me, much Beethoven, much Joyce and (on the latter's theme) Debussy in his *Prélude à l'après-midi d'un faune*, touch real emotions – remind me of emotions I have experienced – in a way that Lawrence does not. Recognizing, as ever, that as others have had different experiences and, in all circumstances, experience themselves differently from me, I nevertheless find Lawrence's reminder of sardine tins as among things that 'can't be ravished' a tiresome irrelevancy. If 'so many women are like that' it must be because they are wearing chastity belts whose keys are lost or may never return from the Crusades. And so many men are 'like that' because (to switch from the strained metaphor) they are invulnerable to being ravished – enclosed in a hard impenetrable casing by over-mothering or feelings of guilt through ignorance, or failure to mature past adolescence. Who ravishes men, though? And how? Perhaps I have already lost confidence in Lawrence as a guide. I get bored similarly with the episodic nature of some of Janacek's music – in his two string quartets for example.

When Joyce describes, in the character of Stephen Dedalus, the wish to be touched when lonely it is all of a piece. That soft eyes touch one in one way and a soft soft soft hand in another is an example of the play of punning akin to music, at which Joyce excels: we are at once reminded that loneliness results not merely from a lack of physical contact but of a communication of feeling, of *true* sympathy.

Lawrence, with all his pretended interest in the ravishing of the earth fails to transcend 'dead words become obscene'. He word-spins, albeit on worthy themes, much as Hindemith seems often to note-spin on dead themes and sequences. By contrast Molly Bloom, an earth-mother, roves in her soliloquy over the real ground of her being and ours. If there is a tinge of jealousy in the passage I have quoted the reader perceives it in a context moving towards Molly Bloom's ultimate fulfilment – '. . . and his heart was going like mad and yes I said yes I will Yes'.

Of course I've been grossly unfair to Lawrence. His purpose is not the same as Joyce's. He seeks to convey the idea of tenderness through barriers of class language and explicitness down to earth. Joyce is using language to explore the tenderness in the Earth (Mother) from the inside. So Joyce can present also her roughness, whereas Connie is

26

relatively cardboard and the roughnesses Lawrence portrays are all outside her. It is as if Lawrence's logic progressed from his *need* for Frieda, his wife (who clearly shared certain significant characteristics with the fictional Connie) to his consequential love for her: as this need never diminished he could not accept her roughness, and his own with her, as an inevitable part of their relationship. He knew the truth of this though he could not acknowledge it. Hence the note on which Mellors' soliloquy (in a letter to Connie who is expecting their baby and awaits her divorce) ends *Lady Chatterly's Lover*: 'But a great deal of us is together, and we can abide by it, and steer our courses to meet soon. John Thomas says good-night to Lady Jane, a little droopingly, but with a hopeful heart'; and in a sentence a few paragraphs before that: 'Well, so many words, because I can't touch you.'

This diversion into a literary comparison is *à propos* art as a reminder to the emotions. In literature, especially in poetry, it is not just the words which serve the communication of meaning but what lies between and among them. As Joyce is the supreme master in the English language of what I have called 'the play of punning akin to music', so what in music moves and touches us is the play of music akin to punning. We don't read a sad novel 'because' we are sad or 'in order to' make us sad but rather (among many other possible reasons) to be reminded, through the depiction of a sad fictional experience, of the universality of the emotion.

If life were all sadness, guilty feelings and hopelessness there could be little to live for; but if it were all happiness and fulfilment how could one value one's good fortune? As there is so wide and subtle a range of emotional response to life perceived through the senses but experienced too often through conditioning and not directly, it is healthy to have and we should welcome opportunities to be reminded of emotions within that range. An inspired choice of music might be a compact reflection of an inner conversation. 'I would like to be reminded of autumnal wistfulness – so I will play a record of Elgar's cello concerto'; or 'Debussy's *La Mer* will remind me of the sea's restless moods, like my own just now'; or 'As I'm feeling rather resentful I should recall the virtue of stoicism expounded in Beethoven's last string quartet ("Must it be?", "It must be") Opus 135.' In reality, we will not generally choose what to listen to, even when we *can* thanks to the convenience of recorded music, on the basis of anything so specific and deliberate. Nor as a rule will we be put off listening to whatever the radio chances to offer, or fail to book for a concert in case some item in the programme might conflict with an unforseeable mood when the time comes.

In an article[5] to introduce a BBC International Festival of Light Music, Steve Race referred to 'the greatness of someone like Ivor Novello, who poured out heart-stopping tunes as if from a bottomless well, but probably never wrote in his life what formal musicians call "a development section". In that respect he differs from symphonic composers like Sibelius or for that matter Beethoven, whose melodic themes, however fine in themselves, are ultimately vehicles for the discussion process.'

Some of us appreciate 'the discussion process' especially. Others seem to be quite content with plenty of tunes. Busoni can sacrifice tunes to an obsession with the discussion process (as in his piano concerto) while, for me, Bruckner spoils some of his most promising melodic material with long-winded and repetitious 'discussion' of it. Others, it seems are not impelled, as I have been sometimes, to vote for Bruckner with the off switch, finding his melodies and discussion quite simply beautiful.

So Bruckner won't go away: he evidently suits many listeners, constituted differently from me. I write from the premise of the universal significance of music as, for certain purposes, an essential food. No more than clues to that significance will be found in the work of any particular composer, nor are such clues to be found only in music itself or the analysis of or commentary upon music.

To enter a record shop is to enter a man's world – some eighty per cent of the customers for classical works are men. Why should this be so? Answers to this question are, at best, speculative. Do women spend more time window-shopping and more money on personal adornment, so as to look, more often than not, 'their best' and to keep up with commercially orientated changing fashions? Men, traditionally (for two hundred years or so, in our society) troubled rather less about how they looked, what visual impact they made on others; variety and choice were narrowed to the evidence of hair on the face and the colour and possibly the significance of the tie or, if no tie were worn, the colour and cut of the shirt. Youths may nowadays be more interested in their appearances than their female counterparts; perhaps that explains, partly at least, decreasing sales of classical recordings to the public.

Listening to music otherwise than at a concert is a relatively unsocial activity. Even teenagers with their personal hi-fis are deliberately cutting themselves off from aural communication with fellow humans encountered on their travels, though this is only an extension of the general denial of identity, between strangers and between mere visual acquaintances, in city life today, to which I have already referred. Do men prefer to hide themselves in a collection of recordings which are waiting to be heard, where women loosen and then lose themselves in small talk? Is listening to music for a man his way of experiencing his emotions, inwardly, where a woman will more readily and naturally express and expose her feelings as they occur?

We men, looking for new records, new recordings to add to our collections, seem to be searching for something of lesser or no concern to women. In Jungian terms a man, in his search to recognize and come to be in balance with his *anima*, the 'dark' or hidden side of his being, may aim to satisfy his romantic yearnings through listening to music, where a woman looks for her *animus* in the visual imagery of a romantic novel or film. A man traditionally identifies with *macho* pursuits – fighting, sport, motor-bikes and cars and other beautiful technical achievements (such as cameras and computers) while a woman, according to unreliable male chauvinists, identifies with a new hair-do, an article of clothing or piece of jewellery, her kitchen, her home, 'her' children. It might be argued that men are happiest with things that *work* well – a locally conventional attitude to other people, politics (but when *do* they work?), a piece of machinery or a piece of music; women, for comparison, are happiest with whatever contributes to attractive appearances, though if it works well too, so much the better.

These generalizations are certainly not of universal application; they exist and flourish within the gradually changing dynamic of relationships between the sexes. And those relationships themselves reflect a gradually changing, it may be developing, it may be evolving, relationship within individuals of each sex – a man with his *anima*, a woman with her *animus*. It is not my concern to examine the implications of these considerations for the recording industry. I mention them because they fascinate me as unexplored territory in which to theorize in the absence of the necessary information to

29

explain the known phenomena; and because they constitute one of the mysteries at the heart of my enquiry.

---

[1] *Beethoven*, OUP, 1944, p.73; c.f. p.80, 'Whether a movement has one theme or half a dozen, whether its texture is polyphonic or homophonic – all such questions tell us as little about the real capacity of a work as the way in which a horse's mane is clipped tells us of its capacity on a race-course.'
[2] D. H. Lawrence, *Lady Chatterly's Lover*, Penguin Books, 1960, p.97.
[3] *Ulysses*, John Lane, The Bodley Head, 1937, p.45.
[4] ibid. p.726.
[5] *Radio Times*, 2–8 June 1979.

4

'WITH ALL THE CHOICEST MUSIC...'[1]

Vaughan Williams, for his *Serenade to Music* composed for Sir Henry Wood's jubilee concert at the Albert Hall in 1938, chose and edited exceptionally evocative lines from the fifth act of *The Merchant of Venice*:

Lorenzo: How sweet the moonlight sleeps upon this bank!
   Here will we sit and let the sounds of music
   Creep in our ears; soft stillness and the night
   Become the touches of sweet harmony.
   . . . Look how the floor of heaven
   Is thick inlaid with patines of bright gold;
   There's not the smallest orb which thou behold'st
   But in his motion like an angel sings,
   Still quiring to the young-ey'd cherubins;
   Such harmony is in immortal souls.
   But whilst this muddy vesture of decay
   Doth grossly close it in, we cannot hear it.
   Come, Lo! and wake Diana with a hymn;
   With sweetest touches pierce your mistress' ear,
   And draw her home with music.
Jessica: I am never merry when I hear sweet music.
Lorenzo: The reason is your spirits are attentive;

> . . . The man that hath no music in himself,
> Nor is not mov'd with concord of sweet sounds,
> Is fit for treasons, stratagems, and spoils;
> The motions of his spirit are dull as night,
> And his affections dark as Erebus.
> Let no such man be trusted.
> . . .

Portia: . . . Music! Hark!
Nerissa: It is your music . . . of the house.
Portia: . . . Methinks it sounds much sweeter than by day.
Nerissa: Silence bestows that virtue on it . . .
Portia: How many things by seasons season'd are
> To their right praise and true perfection!
> Peace, ho! The moon sleeps with Endymion,
> And would not be awak'd.

The words '. . . soft stillness and the night become the touches of sweet harmony' are repeated at the end to round off the composer's, and Shakespeare's sensitive reflection upon the power of music.

As so often in his plays, Shakespeare seems to be referring here to three distinct, interconnected levels of music's influence.

First, silence is said to render the sound of music sweeter, as in the 'soft stillness of night'. So to appreciate music best and to hear it in its 'true perfection' one should listen to it at the right time, on the right occasion (in Hamlet's words, 'ripeness is all') and in the right company, as in Fitzgerald's *Rubaiyat of Omar Khayyam*:

> Here with a loaf of Bread beneath the Bough,
> A flask of wine, a Book of Verse – and Thou
> Beside me singing in the Wilderness –
> And Wilderness were Paradise enow;

or as Lorenzo has it:

> How sweet the moonlight sleeps upon this bank!
> Here will we sit and the sounds of music
> Creep in our ears . . .

Secondly, Jessica is never merry when she hears sweet music and

Lorenzo tells her that is because her 'spirits are attentive'. ('Merry'? –
'. . . and, in a merry sport, if you repay me not on such a day . . . let the
forfeit be nominated for an equal pound of your fair flesh . . .' says
Shylock, Act I Scene 3, seeking Antonio's friendship, even his love,
when urging him to accept, interest free, the loan he needs and inviting
him to go to a notary 'to seal a single bond'.) Lorenzo explains that 'a
wild and wanton herd . . . of youthful and unhandled colts, Fetching
mad bounds, bellowing and neighing loud, Which is the hot condition
of their blood; If they but hear perchance a trumpet sound, Or any air
of music touch their ears . . . make a mutual stand, their savage eyes
turn'd to a modest gaze By the sweet power of music.' When one's
'spirits are attentive' to the sounds of sweet music one cannot remain
boisterous, be 'merry'. It is as if the act of giving attention to music
draws one's energy out of fecklessness. In contrast, in the absence of
attentiveness – '. . . this muddy vesture of decay Doth grossly close it in,
we cannot hear it'. In *Shylock's End*,[2] one of the several Shakespearean
plays performed on the radio, which my father wrote in the last years of
his life, Shylock is approaching his death, after his conversion to
Christianity. Before he dies he is united in mutual forgiveness with his
former adversaries and is full of understanding gratitude to Portia, his
'Daniel', for having, as he has eventually come to see, by an ostensibly
cruel trick delivered him from three poisonous 'snakes' – Hatred,
Greed and Pride. Shakespeare had Tubal, a Jew and a friend of
Shylock, blame himself and other friends for egging Shylock on to
avenge all their grievances on a single enemy seemingly in his power –
'Shylock went mad, and only then remembered the "merry bond" . . .
We fed his madness.' Antonio comments 'All hatred is made. And
hatred, it seems, is in all of us – and the scapegoat pays!' When 'spirits
are attentive' need one be miserable when one cannot be merry? May
not 'sweet music' penetrate such 'madness'?

Thirdly, in writing of the motion of 'the smallest orb which thou
behold'st . . . like an angel sings . . . Such harmony is in immortal souls,'
Shakespeare recalls Plato describing the harmony of the spheres –
celestial music: and one is reminded also, as Plato may have been, of
the Book of Job – 'The morning stars sang together.'[3]

Where did Plato, Shakespeare or anyone else pick up this extraordinary
idea of music made by and between the heavenly bodies? Shakespeare

has a passing reference in *Twelfth Night* (Act III Scene 1); and in *Pericles*, Prince of Tyre (in that latter part of the play which is attributed to him) there is a most curious exchange (Act V Scene 1) just as Pericles discovers his long-lost daughter Marina, whose mother died at her birth:

Pericles: . . . I am wild in my beholding.
　O heavens bless my girl! But, hark, what music?
　Tell Helicanus, my Marina, tell him
　O'er, point by point, for yet he seems in doubt,
　How sure you are my daugher. But, what music?
Helicanus: My lord, I hear none.
Pericles: None!
　The music of the spheres! List, my Marina.
Lysimachus: It is not good to cross him; give him way.
Pericles: Rarest sounds! Do ye not hear?
Lysimachus: My lord, I hear.　　　　　　　　　　　　[Music]
Pericles: Most heavenly music!
　It nips me into listening, and this slumber
　Hangs upon mine eyes: let me rest.　　　　　　　[Sleeps]

The Goddess Diana then appears to Pericles in a dream. She bids him to tell everyone the stories of his and his daughter's adversities: 'Do it, and happy; by my silver bow!'

It hardly stretches the 'action' too far to suggest that Pericles was in a trance when he heard 'the music of the spheres'. In the not dissimilar last scene of *The Tempest*, Prospero, before Miranda, *his* daughter, and his son, are restored to him, describes evidence of his 'rough magic' powers which he declares he intends immediately to abjure, adding: '. . . and, when I have required Some heavenly music, – which even now I do, – To work mine end upon their senses, that This airy charm is for, I'll break my staff . . .' – his wand. And Prospero's aim? 'Now my charms are all o'erthrown, and what strength I have's mine own, Which is most faint . . . Now I want Spirits to enforce, art to enchant; And my ending is despair Unless I be relieved by prayer, Which pierces so, that it assaults Mercy itself, and frees all faults. As you from crimes would pardon'd be, Let your indulgence set me free.'

Shakespeare's purpose finds a contemporary echo in *The Tao of Physics*,[4] a book in which the author Fritjof Capra, a physicist, explores the correspondence between the theories of atomic and subatomic physics and mystical traditions of the East. He commends, for the survival of our civilization, no less, a cultural revolution which will depend on our ability 'to experience the wholeness of nature and the art of living with it in harmony'. We are ever in the presence of the – to us inaudible – 'music of the spheres', if we would 'realize' this truth.

Down to earth, though, where does this connect with the music we can hear all around us daily? I have introduced the idea of the sense in which it can, *but not on the verbal level*, remind us of inner yearnings, tensions, resolutions. As string quartet writing developed from its initial flowering in the works of Haydn and Mozart, conversation or interplay between four potentially equal instruments – that is between four instruments each of which can, if the composer chooses, make an equivalent contribution – enables inner voices in harmony or counterpoint to involve one beyond the surface tune or obvious argument. This has not ceased to be one of the major glories of the string quartet, enabling it to express grandeur and subtlety, universality and intimacy, joy and grief, into the twentieth century: through Fauré, Franck, Sibelius, Ravel, Debussy to Robert Simpson, Segerstam and Bartok, Elliott Carter (in the footsteps of Ives' bold experimentation) and to John Harvey, Ferneyhough, Scelsi, Xenakis and Holliger, through Schoenberg, Berg and Webern to Ligeti and Lutoslawski.

We hear always much more than we listen to.[5] Just as the timbre of an instrument, the sound distinguishing it from any other which is playing the 'same' note, depends on the peculiar blend of its unique overtones, so it is the blend *in motion* of the individual instruments in a string quartet – or indeed in an orchestra or any other ensemble – playing a particular combination of notes which governs the music's influence on the listener's mood: different for each listener and different each time each listener listens. That is hardly surprising. Neither I nor anyone else is 'the same person' exactly, twice in a lifetime. To quote Aaron Copland: '. . . if it is a great work of art, don't expect it to mean exactly the same thing to you each time you return to it'.[6]

In other words music feeds into the complex computer of a listener's mind a range and a *mélange* of messages, stimulating a series and a mingling of formulated, half-formulated and unformulated responses some of which may continue to resonate for some while after the sounds have faded. So may sexual stimulation, for man and woman, be experienced on each occasion differently. The analogy may be followed in a number of directions.

We may see ourselves as fortunate to live in a musically extravagant and heterogeneous society. A completely catholic taste is admirable or so regarded except among those (including me) who lack it; it is admirable, that is, if it is not merely superficial, i.e. unknowledgeable, unable to apply qualitative criteria, lacking care or ability to discriminate between relatively 'good' and relatively 'bad' in each musical category.

Some people will appear to remain satisfied throughout their lives with a narrow range of music. Others never cease to extend their experience in (for them) new music or different performances of familiar music. This is one of those delightful examples of human variety the benefits of which, to everyone else, I would extol.

Although the analogy of sexual relationships and musical experience may be followed it should not be pressed too far. In the field of listening which we are exploring I am treating the art of listening as an active, i.e. non-passive activity. I am concerned with its effects on the listener. It may be assumed that reciprocity is absent, as if it must resemble masturbation whereby one's own action must suffice to give a measure of 'satisfaction' or consolation. But in reality the feedback, even in the case of a familiar recording may be less predictable – or otherwise less acceptable until boredom frustrates altogether even a residual point in playing it.

In the indulgence of musical promiscuity 'disengagement' at that point is generally painless, no one else being involved, no one else's feeling having been involved, there is no hurtful jilting, no walking-out on another, no fear of broken hearts or dishes. Nobody is likely to mind if you say politely, 'I'm getting a bit tired of that, can't we drop it for a while?' Or less politely, 'Turn the bloody thing off, I'm sick of it.' In contrast a lover or a spouse is traditionally entitled to be at least a little nettled at being 'cast off', turned out, deserted, shared, discarded for someone younger, in a word, humiliated.

If Chopin may be murdered, as they say, so may composers in more sophisticated company, be humiliated, but not, surely, *music* itself.

Furthermore (to pursue the sexual analogy), music, like sex, is experienced through the senses. Though music may be accompanied by the sight of drama or dance and may stimulate movement it must be acknowledged that sex has the edge over music in terms of sense perception since it can evoke a response (of attraction or repulsion) through any one or more or all of the five primary senses, while music, for the listener at least, must make its impact through little else but sound impinging on the sense of hearing. If that were the whole story one might expect music to become boring sooner than sex. No such logical presumption would, however, be justified so far as one can judge in the absence of any research and reliable statistics. I do not believe the comparison is suitable for research or amenable, even if it were, to statistical analysis. (And I regard 'reliable statistics' as virtually self-contradictory.)

Nevertheless there is an interesting analogy between the effects of inevitably non-static sexual relationships – that is relationships in which there is a sexual element of inevitably fluctuating import to the whole relationship – and music from which the stimulation of one's non-verbal intellect and one's emotions and pleasure in movement activates or reactivates certain areas in one's complex computer-mind.

Behind sex and beyond it lies the pre-programmed urge to participate in the perpetuation of the species. Beyond music lies the music of the spheres, and within it lies the capacity to trigger an intuitive feeling for the oneness of all which exists in the universe. However that capacity is apparently attractive to only a small proportion of the music-loving population. Just as a subconscious urge to perpetuate the species is not what men and women generally feel when they want to make love, so an approach to listening to music is made from a variety of motives and from mixed motives. We tend not to bother to observe or formulate our motives for doing anything.

Indeed, it is as if we only imagine that we are awake, 'conscious', knowing and recalling that other state of even deeper sleep, 'sleep with dreams'. It is, then, in a state of relative sleep that a choice appears to be made – of a lover, spouse, musical programme, work or performance. In the low state of consciousness which we regard as our customary 'waking state', each of us is almost invariably without deliberate control of our actions, thoughts and feelings: they occur as automatic reactions to sense perceptions of our computerized minds, conditioned largely by acquired attitudes and responding through a number of distinct pseudo-egos. In this way we *seem* to be genuinely motivated, according to the manner of our reaction to external and internal events through one or another pseudo-ego, to 'make choices'. Hence, more often than not, our choices of music – as of anything else in life. Generally we take for granted the reality of choice: we ignore any evidence of the pressures, some hardly hidden, which often virtually force a particular decision on us. A real choice must, however, be made in *some* circumstances, e.g. when pressures are apparently evenly balanced; or if balancing factors are incompatible for the purpose of comparison (like chalk and cheese); or we realize that we are or will be, at the crucial time, ignorant or uncertain of the likely effects of relevant factors. Then we are uncomfortable, we wriggle, we may speak of being on the 'horns of a dilemma'.

As I was writing the last paragraph my son Adam joined me and I told him that I had, earlier in the evening, written to a Finnish friend who had sent him a gramophone record made by two of her sons with a 'new-wave' or punk group. On the previous day Adam had started to draft a letter to thank her but he was stuck. He said truthfully that he liked the record (it was a lovely colour – 'see-through turquoise green' he called it); but, to be kind, he found the music unattractive or, to be honest, a horrible noise. Just at that time Dvorak's mass in D major, which I had 'chosen' to listen to since it was being broadcast on Radio 3, ended with half an hour left 'to take us to the news', as some Radio 3 announcers infuriatingly persist in saying to comfort listeners. What exactly Adam should write was his dilemma; what (if any) music, lasting no more than half an hour, I should 'play' was mine.

An LP would have been, in my terms, inappropriate but a 60 minute (i.e. 2×30 minute) cassette could be just right. That ruled out all 90 (2×45) minute cassettes. As I intended to set it going without delay I would have to accept whichever of the A or the B side of a cassette was ready to play: that narrowed by fifty per cent my choice of music on 60 minute cassettes which I had recorded off the air (at the time under licence from the Mechanical Copyright Protection Society!). Of those recorded over the previous three months or so (the earlier ones, nearly forgotten, in a drawer) my roving eye landed on the legend for a cassette which struck me as unfamiliar. So I decided to put it on.

A Beethoven piano concerto unexpectedly! I couldn't guess which one, or why my note should be wrong. 'It's Jolyon Brettingham-Smith's *No-set ensemble*,' I told Adam. There followed an extraordinary radio talk, a bit pompous, jargon-filled, gradually expanded by voices-over which sounded like many radio talks of the same kind spoken simultaneously, followed by 'music' which Adam said was like 'The Soft Machine'. It evidently overran the tape and there was no concluding announcement, just as there had been no opening announcement. I removed the cassette and looked at the key: side A, not B! 'Oh! we were listening to Roland Pfrengle's *Thema-Information for flute and tape* or *(Somebody Said) (group improvisation) (first broadcast performance)* and not to the Jolyon Brettingham-Smith.' An example of how to make a perfect choice.

The intrusive beginning of a Beethoven piano concerto, perhaps truly part of Mr Pfrengle's work, was welcome as a pleasant surprise when I was braced for the unusual not the merely unexpected. Some people, in exercising what they regard as choice, will invariably prefer familiar music. In general familiar music may be regarded as easier to listen to than unfamiliar music: we know what is coming and can listen lazily, with half an ear, that is with only partial or spasmodic attention.

We may be less comfortable or even uncomfortable with unfamiliar music according to its style. For listeners as distinct from performers, I suspect that there are roughly two categories – those who prefer to listen to music they have heard before, or music in a similar style, and those who prefer to extend their listening repertoire. The former inevitably sometimes hear music they do not know and thus their 'repertoire' gradually expands. The latter, among whom I include myself, do not cease to hear and to enjoy music heard many times before – but preferably with an unusual feature, perhaps an unusual juxtaposition with other works, or performed by an exceptional artist.

Such factors as these influence to some extent my use of the gramophone. Once I had a collection of 78s which began with some of the orchestral classics I remembered from pre-war concert-going – Beethoven's *Eroica* symphony, an Elgar symphony, Elgar's and Dvorak's cello concertos, Brahms' *St Anthony Variations* and his *German Requiem*, Mahler's *Song of the Earth*, serenades for strings by Dvorak and Elgar, the Mozart concerto for flute and harp and Bach's *Brandenburg* concertos. That was enough to be going on with, but the Third Programme was getting into its stride and increasingly I sought less familiar music on record and turned more to chamber music, particularly string quartets; and while not neglecting Bach, Haydn, Mozart and Beethoven I made a point of acquiring often secondhand, deleted records of 'modern' works some of which have not been returned to the catalogue of LPs, in this country at least.

Among my 'lucky buys' were three string quartets by Malipiero (coincidentally all found on the same day – two at Harridges and one at Collectors' Corner); ancient recordings of Beethoven by the Lener quartet – not, I thought, as good as their reputation; the Flonzaley quartet – a wonderful performance with Harold Bauer of Brahms' piano quintet and which I was delighted to find again, on LP in late 1979; Hindemith's third and Bartok's second string quartets performed by Amar, Caspar, Hindemith and his brother – (Bartok's outer slow movements are played most movingly and the middle movement ultra-fast, but amazingly they botched the second of the two chords with which the work ends); Bloch's first and second quartets and his excellent suite for viola and piano (not the orchestral version); Alan Bush's *Dialectic* quartet, Bloch's and Hindemith's violin concertos. My interest in Stravinsky's wind octet soon palled: to me he is a great composer for his austere *Symphony of Psalms*, for *Rite of Spring* and his (surely too good for ballet) *Les Noces*.

EMG, a London record shop, which I discovered just when I was beginning to collect, for years afterwards provided an invaluable monthly newsletter reviewing and comparing the ever vaster output of new and reissued records. Until the advent of LPs, EMG not only sold hand-made gramophone machines with huge horns and triangular fibre needles to be sharpened with a special pair of scissors, but at that time encouraged customers to listen to records on them. I was additionally fortunate on an early visit to be recommended by a young and intelli-gent assistant to try a newly issued recording of Bartok's fifth string quartet (played by the Hungarian String Quartet). I took it up to a listening room and soon decided that it was 'impossible'. I couldn't even follow it on the score she had lent me, but it transpired that this was because of the collapse of the point on the triangular needle. Anyway my sympathetic guide so believed in the quality of the work that she offered to lend me her set of three records to listen to at my leisure at home. That was enough for me; I promptly bought the work and played it no less than eight times in the first week (without needle breakdown). It was the most exciting 'new music' I had ever heard, imaginative, spare (i.e. no note padding), convincingly argued and extraordinarily beautiful, the sound, the themes, the harmonies gripping throughout. I became a Bartok-bore to my family and friends, my single-track excitement soon after encouraged by my finding the much scratched and worn, set of Bartok's second quartet referred to above.

As I accumulated my first idiosyncratic collection, the 78s, I initiated a practice carried into my second collection, the LPs, of writing the date on the sleeve whenever I played a record. Why? Habit now, of course, but that cannot be all or I should never have started it. The information of the frequency of my patronage of certain kinds of music, specific works and particular performances incidentally tells me how my *assumed* tastes compare with my decision to play my records to satisfy them.

Other gramophone buffs may not need such information to tell them that when a new record joins a collection it is more likely to be played than any other for a week or two: or that it will probably be played three times before another record is played. Then, according to the size of the collection *and* the measure of one's satisfaction with the new acquisition, it may be dropped from the 'repertory' for months or years.

For me this pattern of behaviour is distorted by certain practical factors which I am sure I share with some other 'collectors'. Only gradually have operas entered my collection of LPs. I had no opera on 78s. I found it hard enough to face the need to turn over or replace a record every four and a half minutes or so for string quartet versions of Bach's *Art of Fugue* (Roth) and of Haydn's *Seven Last Words on the Cross* (Griller) and Franck's only string quartet (*Pro Arte*); each had six or more records. As it was my practice then not, if I could help it, to play less than a complete work at one sitting,[7] I was never tempted to acquire any opera on 78s. Besides in those, my prolonged bachelor days, I spent many happy evenings in the amphitheatre, just below 'the gods', at the Royal Opera House, Covent Garden, enjoying the post-war opera boom without having to jump up every few minutes to fix the next side of a record on the turntable.

On LPs I have, over the years, acquired Berlioz' *Les Troyens*, Wagner's *Tristan and Isolde* and *The Ring* (Furtwängler – an old recording but compelling), Mussorgsky's *Boris Godunov* (unspoilt by Rimsky-Korsakov), Verdi's *Aida, Otello* and *Falstaff*, Britten's *Peter Grimes*, Schoenberg's *Moses and Aaron*, Janacek's *Excursions of Mr Broucek*, Berg's *Wozzeck* and *Lulu* (the latter superbly performed under Christoph von Dohnányi – magnificent music sadly without Act III, which was subsequently reconstructed and performed far less impressively under Boulez), Pfitzner's *Palestrina*, Debussy's *Pelléas et Mélisande* and Tippett's *King Priam* and *The Knot Garden* and no less than five versions of Bartok's *Duke Bluebeard's Castle*. No Mozart, no Strauss, no Rossini, Donizetti, Bellini.

It is cruel to inflict any opera on the members of my family not (yet) attuned to my musical taste, at any other than a suitable volume, never too high for comfort. Their tastes are generally unformed or simply different from mine. I am less merciful in the case of shorter works. But in the case of *Lulu* and especially *Moses and Aaron*, with the difficulty of adjusting to the distortion of human voices even on the best hi-fi equipment, which mine is not quite, the twelve-tone idiom is liable to place family love and tolerance in jeopardy. These are powerful arguments against the operas on record or radio which I would myself choose to hear. Additionally, I find tiresome the need for visualization of stage action, where the music or singer fails to command one's attention. For purely musical reasons it is far easier to visualize action in *Peter Grimes* than – at the other end of the scale – *Pelléas et Mélisande*.

There are additional reasons why I seldom wish to listen to recorded or broadcast operas. Often the words cannot be distinguished or understood. Then I decide that the music of itself, even if well-known and well-loved, seldom justifies the dedication of time to listen to a complete opera in one sitting with only natural breaks. Probably that is an excuse: the comprehensibility of words in an opera must, as a rule, be of far less significance than the music. If I could muster the stamina I would prefer even to swallow Wagner's whole *Ring Cycle* in a great gulp, like Balint Vazsonyi's marathon only with more performers and many more notes, though I understand hardly a word of German.

My avoidance of operatic singing spills over to lieder. Perhaps one day I will find it as enjoyable and fascinating as string quartets have been for me for many years. I do, however, rejoice to have in my collection and play once or twice bi-annually, Berlioz' *Nuits d'Été* (several performances), Warlock's *The Curlew*, Britten's *Serenade* for tenor, horn and strings and his *Michelangelo Sonnets*, Ravel's songs (provided they include his *Chansons madécasses*) and Strauss's *Four Last Songs*. I enjoy no less Monteverdi's *Vespers* and innumerable masses and motets by the great sixteenth-century Flemish masters, notably Ockeghem, di Lassus, Josquin des Prés, Obrecht, de la Rue, Dufay and above all of these the Italian Gesualdo, who composed in an harmonic idiom of strikingly 'modern' originality, tormented, it may be, by guilt at having had his wife and her lover murdered.

Without cataloguing my present collection this outline of its scope may explain it in terms of listening choice. It hardly illustrates the peculiarity of a musical taste to add that I would not want to be without, say, Schnabel's old recording of Beethoven's *Diabelli* variations, yet listen to it seldom since acquiring Brendel's more recently recorded 'cooler' performance for contrast. Paradoxically I prefer the Schnabel, though I would not wish to be without Brendel playing Beethoven's *Bagatelles* or his set of the last piano sonatas of Schubert.

When I discover from the list of dates on an envelope, that it is more than two years since I last played a record, I am induced to play it as soon as possible unless I know that I have become bored with the music or am too critical of the performance – good reasons anyway to reject the record for jumble at the next opportunity. Hence my dating habit may distort my vaunted freedom of choice, unless overridden by other factors such as a more positive or pressing desire to hear something else.

And that brings me face to face with crucial elements in the 'choice' of a particular work or performance to play on a particular occasion. Sometimes I am sure too much is made of mood as a deciding factor in the amalgam of subconscious reasoning which results in choice. Too often for my comfortable image of myself as a rational being, choice falls on what comes early to my hand or eye. As my collection is big enough to deny me instant recall of everything in it, only a roving hand or eye will pick out something forgotten without recourse to a mental dredging exercise. Far from regretting such weak evidence of choice I feel glad to be reminded in this random way of a neglected record. The unexpected, unplanned pleasure reinforces the temptation on sub-sequent occasions to repeat this roving method of 'choosing'. It resembles the art of picking a Grand National winner with eyes closed and a pin, except that I cannot claim of the records in my collection 'every one a winner'.

No less cogent to the analysis of 'choice' is the attraction/repulsion mechanism applicable to the familiar rather than the unfamiliar – or *vice versa*, already touched on briefly. Some people have a voracious, even insatiable, appetite for the unfamiliar while others are quite unadventurous. It's a wonder they can put together a collection at all. If I am not to be slavishly persuaded by record reviews, it may be that only regular concert-going is likely to broaden my musical experience vertically in the scale of historical time and horizontally in the music of any particular period or 'school'.

Concert-goers do not mostly stick to concerts of works by only their favourite composers – all Tchaikovsky, all Beethoven, all Chopin; perhaps a dozen or so other composers command such chauvinism. But if their love of the music of any one composer or of the composers of any one period is sincere they are most likely to sit through many concerts without a material extension of their listening experiences. The unknown becomes known and perhaps eventually familiar, even acceptable. It may then join the 'A' list, as it were, of works for which special effort is made to attend performances. To what extent this sequence derives from radio listening, with more or less sympathetic attention, I do not know, but I am sure that music clubs and the records played to 'captive audiences' by their friends are immensely and relevantly influential wherever an adventurous policy is followed, for so long at least as the element of 'captivity' is not resented.

There is nothing to compare with the enthusiasm of someone whose judgement is respected to persuade one to listen with the expectation that one will find a work worth listening to irrespective, perhaps in spite of one's previous prejudice. It is sad that sometimes such enthusiasm is wasted if its target then hears an inferior performance of a recommended work and is put off it 'for life' or until good fortune redresses the wrong. I feel no shame for the many occasions when I brought one or another girlfriend home to listen to records (a music-lover's etchings), handed her the typed list of 78s I kept at the time (cross-indexed for composers and for category of work) and as she excitedly turned the pages – in those days whoever it was loved music – said to her almost brutally, 'Anyway, I'm going to play you this,' making my own choice. I like to think that those choices were 'tailor-made' for my audience of the evening; but I admit that sometimes (maybe often) I put on just what *I* wanted to hear. Perhaps one reason for my prolonged bachelordom in the days of 78s was the inhibitory effect on courtship of my having to jump up every few minutes to keep the music flowing. I was obliged eventually to re-assess my priorities.

With music we are not unlike animals used for 'psychological' experiments. A bad experience with any unfamiliar composer or a poor performance of an unknown work can be as discouraging as an electric shock for a hungry rat or monkey which presses the wrong button. Yet the advice not to be put off completely may itself be entirely misdirected. I refused for years to believe that any encouragement I might be given to persevere with Bruckner's symphonies would not be wasted; he was not for me – I thought. Then I suffered and survived *partial* conversion with Jochum's convincing performances on record.

I have deliberately discussed music as familiar or unfamiliar rather than as 'easy' or 'difficult'. The former concepts are, of course, relatively relative but the latter are *very* relative! I acknowledge, however, that my energy for listening to 'difficult' music (which may nevertheless be familiar, as for instance Elliott Carter's string quartets have become for me) is sometimes lacking. At times I may positively decide to listen to something 'easy', say a Berwald or Nielsen string quartet, which may be unfamiliar, its choice based securely on assumptions about the composer, his 'school' or the period in which he lived, or hearsay.

Like most people, I am amazingly ignorant about the different energies needed for one activity or another, about the drains on our energies and the best means to restore them. If I run a hundred yards (never mind metres) as fast as I can, whether in or out of training, I shall pant to replace oxygen used as fuel for the exceptional muscular activity. But if I am weary from a stressful day at my office panting will not overcome my fatigue. To listen to music I regard as 'easy' rather than 'difficult', or *vice versa*, after a burst of muscular exertion will be simply irrelevant to my condition. After especially tiring mental activity I might be materially refreshed by jogging round the block and *then* panting but I have not yet tested this hypothesis.

To relax listening to any music may, in *certain* circumstances, 'recharge one's batteries' – but, so far as I am aware, there has not yet been an attempt at objective research into *what* music will restore energy to *which* individuals, having *what* combination of relevant characteristics, when wearied by *what* exertions. And the ambience for relaxation will, I suspect, be found to be a most relevant factor. To listen to music in the company of a relaxed person who is *sympathique* to oneself and also to the music are factors of the utmost significance to me. In other words the context in which relaxation of a certain kind is possible is probably (as I won't try country-and-western I cannot be sure) more important than the choice of music. And the macro-context is no less than the universe itself.

---

[1] Shakespeare's *King Henry VIII*, Act IV, Scene 1.

[2] Harold F. Rubinstein, Gollancz, 1971.

[3] Job 38:7.

[4] Wildwood House, 1975; Fontana, 1976.

[5] See 'The Esoteric World of Sound and Research into Harmonies', Chapter 3 in *Through Music to the Self* by Peter Michael Hamel (trans. Peter Lemesurier), Compton Press, Tisbury, Wiltshire, 1978.

[6] See Chapter 2, page 13.

[7] 'We shall never understand a work of art unless we take it as a whole' (Tovey, *Beethoven*, op.cit. p.15).

5

PIPES AND LYRES

In the beginning was the – word, Brahma; breath, Atman; universal rhythm, OM MANE PADME HUM HROH.[1]

At Nippon Medical University near Tokyo, Professor Hajime Merooka recorded a mother-to-be's body-beat within her womb by the baby's head. The long-playing record of these sounds, *Lullaby Inside Mum*, comforts crying babies. I have not heard it played but it is said to include also 'Sound from Aorta', 'Sound from Aorta and Vein', and 'Womb Sound with *Traumerei*' (Schumann's). Should it surprise anyone that, like mother's milk, mother's sound is best for infants? Let it be in every baby's home – where the equipment and electricity is also available, so that it may be played on demand when the little one is restless. Or, to free parents from the stress of the sound of crying, why not have it on all the time? The universal tranquillizer may prove to be no more addictive than a baby's dummy; in any case mothers need no longer sing their babies to sleep. A lullaby, hummed or with the simplest of reassuring words to accompany a gentle tune must be one of the earliest uses of music, replaceable now by a wonderful medico-scientific discovery, awaiting only commercial exploitation.

There may be good reason for gratitude to Professor Merooka and the Toshiba Music Company if a generation raised on the charms of more urgent rhythms of the free-style disco dance has lost the instinctive ability to sing a lullaby. But instinct may not so quickly be lost. The tremendous, if artificially prompted, popularity of listening to the latest hits, seems to promote all the pleasure of singing among their fans. It may be that scientists have not yet discovered or invented anything more effective than instincts.

After infancy, deliberately made sounds in primitive communities will have served to summon those within hearing to assemble or to communicate a message where a shout might be lost or misunderstood. Such use is still commemorated on the most solemn occasions in Jewish worship when a ram's horn, the *shofar*, is blown in the synagogue. In other communities a signal may be given by hitting a resonating object, a hollow tree-trunk, a drum; later still a metal object free to vibrate – eventually a gong or bell. Such instruments have been known and used throughout historical time and from their very simplicity, as surviving evidence confirms, were employed in pre-historic societies too. Only gradually in recent years have they been superseded, but still only to a small degree, by similar electronic noises.

Meanwhile a variety of objects capable of use for communication, strictly non-musical though not necessarily un-musical, has spilled over into the world of composed music. Increasingly in this century composers have exploited the huge range of timbre, colour, and effects to be derived from the 'kitchen department' – the percussion section of an orchestra. The triangle is perhaps the simplest instrument of all – in two parts, a three-sided arrangement of bent solid metal tubing slightly open at one corner, held suspended from a band of leather (or string would do) and struck with a hand-held metal rod. While the triangle tinkles or pings, a pair of cymbals, brass plates nowadays of no definite pitch, may be banged together to give a clashing sound: or one alone may be tapped or stroked. (The piano is a sophisticated percussive instrument of some complexity and therefore untypical.)

Such simple instruments are toys to give pleasure to any child. In musical rehearsal and performance they can illustrate a curious distinction of degree between percussive and other methods of producing music – that a more conscious, a more pronounced allowance must be made for delay between the start of the hitting movement and the hit which will produce the sound. It may be that the percussionist with the cymbals has only one occasion to play them – to bash them together – in the course of a whole concert. He will, to be sure, be utterly exposed when the time comes; with the conductor's punctilious assistance he will be reminded anyway when he is to 'come in'. Knowledgeable members of the audience who take pleasure in visual participation will watch as he rises, lifts his heavy cymbals, twists them to face each other, and then adjusts their distance apart according to the required volume of sound to be produced ('dynamics'); the movement of the player's extended but still bent arms to bring the cymbals together must begin a split-second before the essentially precise moment when they are due to clash. The sound reverberates but it is the preparation for the exact timing of impact which requires more than an unpractised child's – or adult's – skill.

In contrast the sounds of wind instruments and stringed instruments, either plucked or bowed, may be regarded as made instantaneously (the organ, though strictly a wind instrument, is a noble exception owing to the nature of its construction). But for these also, precision of timing of each note – which may be sustained at will except in the case of plucked strings – together with dynamics and the individual instruments' peculiarities – is no less crucial, whether in an ensemble or in solo performance, to the quality, that is the musicality of a performance. The listener's conscious and unconscious expectations – in relation to every factor in a performance of a musical work, every note, every combination and sequence of notes in relation to each other, horizontally with a melody in time and vertically with counterpoint and harmony, the distinctive timbre of each instrument derived from its characteristic harmonics – determine his eventual sense of satisfaction with the performance. And satisfaction may be derived from expectations fulfilled or from surprise where they were misplaced or absent.

After a child's first experience with sounds made by hitting or scraping different objects – on parts of his own body or anything else – he may be shown or discover the variety of sounds which can be made by blowing through hollow tubes or past a vibrating membrane such as a blade of grass held taut between thumbs. Did an idle shepherd first find how to make a note with a length of bamboo, hollowed reed or elderberry twig and then go on to try similar tubes of different lengths or thicknesses? History will not tell us how long it must have been, after the first blown note was sounded before a set of pan-pipes was constructed, and how long again before a series of holes along the length of a single tube was found to render the performance of a tune a matter of agile co-ordination of lungs, lips and fingers.[2]

Were the parents of Pan the gods of shepherds and of hunters? In his invaluable historical account, *Heathen Gods and Heroes*, William King records several alternative rumours. My favourite concerns Penelope and Mercury. Their union was said to have been consummated when Mercury came upon Penelope watching over her father's flocks and 'fell in love with her, and finding no other way to obtain her, changed himself into the shape of a very handsome white Goat, and so far prevailed, that she brought him a Son called Pan, who had Horns upon his Head, and the Beard and Feet of a Goat'. (What can Penelope have been thinking to allow even a very handsome white Goat to prevail? Could she have mistaken the Goat for the god?)

William King goes on to tell of Pan, wrapped, new-born, in the skin of a goat, carried into Heaven by his father Mercury, where he immediately 'shewed his Skill in Musick, to the wonder and Delight of all the Gods and afterwards they made him their Messenger, as well as his Father Mercury'. Nymphs of Arcadia contributed to Pan's education: 'And when he grew up he recalled that Favour and used constantly to dance with them, and divert them with the Musick of his Pipe, and wherever they went, to place himself at their Head, as their Conductor.' Pan was apparently susceptible to the 'Passion of Love'. He descended 'from the Heaven into Arcadia and became a Shepherd and Servant to a mortal Man, the Father of Drycope, with whom he was enamoured to the last degree. The Flocks were so delighted with the Musick of his Pipe, that it contributed to the increase of their Milk in great abundance.' (What magnificent symbolism is buried transparently in the myth!)

Some of Pan's exploits in man's wars from Greece to India and back to Spain, are described by William King who also lists numerous amorous conquests for which Pan could show himself as cunning as Jupiter in his use of deception. He did not always succeed. He is said to have had 'a Contention with Cupid, in which he was overcome, whereupon the little God forc'd him to fall in Love with the Nymph Syrinx, who fled from him with Disdain; her Flight was stopp'd by a River, upon which she prayed to the Nacades for Relief: They caus'd a sudden Change, so that when he thought he had hold of her, he embrac'd only a Parcel of Reeds. These Reeds, as he sat fighting and contemplating them on the Banks of the River Ladon, being moved by the Wind and sending forth a gentle Sound, gave him the Thought of imitating it, and forming them into that Pipe, for which he afterwards became so famous.'

Am I too prosaic to imagine a prototype of the mythical Pan as a loner, dressed in ragged, shaggy skins, living in a cave half way up a mountain, an outsider to the Society of Sociable Shepherds of Arcadia? When disturbed or harried he would frighten trespassers to his parish with a mighty yell. Sometimes he would descend for a frolic with the shepherdesses. One long lustful chase led him into a swamp in the valley; for consolation (perhaps his quarry ran too fast for him – or drowned before he could rape her) he cut himself reeds for a pipe and strummed on a random handful as he danced back to his upholstered pad. Over Palaeolithic centuries there would have been very many examples of outcasts leading such lives, some of them spastics, some simpletons; and possibly some of them sages, but that would be untypical. Translated from skins to feathers our Pan was surely epitomized as Papageno in Mozart's opera *The Magic Flute*.

Papageno, with his crude but to him satisfying pipes and all the limitations of an earthbound spirit, stretched upwards. As a decoy bird he knew himself in truth to be a wingless wonder. Tamino, his hero and master, performed another role in the Scheme of the Perfect Playwright (to Freemasons, the Archetype Architect). His natural musical-magical instrument was the subtler flute, a gift of his true anima, Pamina (but really from her wicked mother the Queen of the Night), carved by her father from an ancient oak, which had itself survived many battles with the elements. Papageno is given, for protection, a relatively crude instrument of less potent magic, a set of lightly strung bells.

A major charm for lovers of *The Magic Flute* is uncertainty as to which of the older generation, Sarastro or his former wife the Queen of the Night (saddled with cruelly exposed coloratura arias in the upper regions of, hopefully, a heavenly voice), is the true Baddy and which the true Goody. A dilemma unresolved, for me, even by the Freudian clues presented in *Amadeus*.[3] Mozart's own prevarication is excusable if unknowingly he borrowed their curious history from traces of a story told centuries later by Robert Graves[4] as to how Apollo killed the satyr Marsyas, a follower of the goddess Cybele. Once Athene made a double-flute from stag's bones, and played on it at a banquet of the

51

gods. Her music seemed to delight all but two of the deities. In a huff she went away by herself and, playing the flute again beside a stream, watched her image in the water. Feeling that her bluish face and swollen cheeks made her look ludicrous, she threw down the flute, and laid a curse on anyone who picked it up. Marsyas stumbled upon the flute, the innocent victim of this curse. When he put it to his lips it played of itself, delighting the Phrygian peasants. They cried out that Apollo himself could not have made better music, even on his lyre, and Marsyas foolishly did not contradict them. This provoked the anger of Apollo, who invited him to a contest, the winner of which should inflict whatever punishment he pleased on the loser. Marsyas consented, and Apollo impanelled the Muses as a jury. The contest proved an equal one, the Muses being charmed by both instruments. So cunning Apollo challenged Marsyas to turn his instrument upside down, and both play and sing at the same time. This, with a flute, was of course impossible, and Marsyas failed to meet the challenge. But Apollo reversed his lyre, and sang such delightful hymns in honour of the Olympian gods that the Muses were obliged to give him their verdict. Then, for all his pretended sweetness, Apollo took a cruel revenge on Marsyas: flaying him alive and nailing his skin to a tree.

Revenge for what? We may wonder. In one of his admirable notes, Robert Graves rationalizes this myth as follows:[5] 'Apollo's victories over Marsyas and Pan commemorate the Hellenic conquests of Phrygia and Arcadia, and the consequent supersession in those regions of wind instruments by stringed ones, except among the peasantry. Marsyas's punishment may refer to the ritual flaying of a sacred king – as Athene stripped Pallas of his magical aegis – or the removal of the entire bark from an alder-shoot, to make a shepherd's pipe . . .' And so on.

Titian's *Flaying of Marsyas* was the subject of an article in *The Times*[6] when the painting was shown at the Royal Academy's Venetian exhibition early in 1984. The erudite and perceptive writer quoted an invocation to Apollo from Dante's *Divine Comedy*:

> Come into my heart, and so breathe
> As you did when you extracted Marsyas
> From the skin in which his limbs were enclosed.

He went on to explain 'These strange lines' to 'take full account both of the extreme violence of the act, and of the way the whole passage seems to merge it into the gentle process of divine guidance, inspiration or possession, which the poet is praying for. The image draws on several relevant ideas, but the strongest one is that the relationship between God and the artists, and by extension between God and man, is in some sense like a flaying. The cast of mind which could make such an association may seem very remote – as far as possible from milk-and-water piety. Upside down and amazed, humiliated to the utmost degree, the shaggy satyr has come face to face with God, who is most tenderly and painfully stripping away the bestial side of him.'

Of course there was a no less erudite correspondent at hand to cap Dante. Professor Hugh Lloyd-Jones wrote from Christ Church, Oxford[7] to quote from Edgar Wind's *Pagan Mysteries in the Renaissance*[8] where, he says, the symbolism of the flaying episode is fully worked out: 'The cruelty inflicted on Marsyas by Apollo . . . expresses the supreme sense of disproportion by which the god attacks the human frame, which is agonized as it succumbs to the divine ecstasy.' I am not sure that I do not prefer what Professor Lloyd-Jones called the *Times*' leader writer's 'correct explanation' of the symbolism, even if it was not so fully worked out.

The symbolism of the myth of what he called the 'gloomy mystery' of Marsyas is itself so tortured that it will bear yet a little more light thrown on it by another quotation from Edgar Wind's essay: 'The musical contest between Apollo and Marsyas was . . . concerned with the relative powers of Dionysian darkness and Apollonian clarity; and if the contest ended with the flaying of Marsyas, it was because flaying was itself a Dionysian rite, a tragic ordeal of purification by which the ugliness of the outward man was thrown off and the beauty of his inward self revealed . . . The cry: "Why do you tear me from myself?" expresses then an agonized ecstasy and could be turned, as it was by Dante, into a prayer addressed to Apollo: "Enter my breast, and so infuse me with your spirit as you did Marsyas when you tore him from the cover of his limbs" ' (the same lines from the *Divine Comedy* as were quoted in a different translation in *The Times*).

It would completely confuse Mozart's intentions to equate Tamino with sometimes deceitful Apollo, as the inventor and thus the god of Music. William King refers to Apollo, in this connection (but surely without Marsyas in mind), as having 'found out music as a Comfort and Remedy for the Calamities of human life, being able to excite or allay all the Passions of Mankind, the Muses therefore were under his Protection, he being their President at least, if not their Father; even the Grasshopper, for being a musical Animal, was sacred to him . . .' President at least, of the Muses, if not their Father: *that* is, for sure, not Tamino. But one should not believe all the malicious gossip in circulation about the Greek gods. Many lesser immortals and mortals must have been jealous of their powers if not of their power, of their peccadillos if not of their virtues. But for Mozart the power of music was to attune and to bring into harmony discordant and clashing souls.

There remains an interesting point of comparison between Papageno and Tamino on the one hand and Pan and Apollo on the other. The obvious distinctions should not be allowed to obscure the essential roles of Papageno and Pan to illustrate a striving upwards from the level of Earth; and of Tamino and Apollo to bring a quality of spirit down from the level of Heaven. The esoteric symbol which comes to mind is that variously known as the Seal of Solomon or the Star of David, a six-pointed star composed of two equal triangles, one superimposed upside-down over the other – ⬡ or ✡. Without pursuing an analogy *ad infinitum*, where this one belongs, a flute may be recognized as a developed, refined form of the pipe of Pan; a lyre or lute may be an instrument of another order of sublimity.

No wonder then that Apollo gave a lyre to his son Orpheus, a student of the sacred mysteries in Egypt. The lyre, however, did not enable Orpheus to recover his wife Euridice from the depths of Hades, to which she had been obliged to descend on dying from the bite of a serpent while seeking to escape the unwelcome erotic attentions of Aristeus. This suggests a limitation of the power of even the most sublime music. As Monteverdi's *La Favola d'Orfeo* evidenced, Orpheus yielded to temptation under severe psychological provocation, and Euridice consequently had to descend again. Gluck in his *Orfeo ed Euridice*, composed for a festival occasion – the Austrian Emperor Francis I's name-day in 1762, had to compromise with a happy ending when Amore revives Euridice so as to restore her to the joys of love. (*Amore*: 'All shadow of suffering whatsoever melts away, when I want it to . . . Always rejoice and be grateful to Love!')

A music-lover may know Orpheus best from Monteverdi and Gluck, or from Offenbach's operetta of 1858, *Orpheus in the Underworld*. He might, however, have heard of, if not actually heard, settings of the myth by Purcell or Liszt or possibly Jacopo Peri's *Euridice* (1600), arguably the oldest complete opera to survive; or operas by Rossi, Keiser, Naumann or Krenek, who are for most of us but names in dictionaries of music, and Milhaud (*Les Malheurs d'Orfée*) or Malipiero of whom we should have heard; and no doubt many others too.

In another myth, however, it seems that Orpheus was Dionysus, who, as Robert Graves put it, 'played the rude alder-pipe, not the civilized lyre'. Therein lies another example of correspondencies at intervals, as it were, on a scale of spiritual development, comparable to the chemical table of valencies.

A wooden flute seems specially honoured (although nowadays flutes are commonly made of metal). Krishna captivated the Gopis, milk-maidens with whom he sported in his youth, with a wooden flute. According to a narrative poem, *King Cole*, by the poet laureate John Masefield OM, the ghost of that saintly king played a flute to miraculous effect in the reign of Queen Victoria.[9]

There are however many other instruments to which magical powers have been attributed, including the Pied Piper of Hamelin's pipe (in a recent opera by Hugo Cole and a slightly earlier one by Anthony Smith-Masters), the bagpipe (*Svanda Dudak* by Htilmay; and Weinberger's better known work *Svanda the Bagpiper*), the violin (Stravinsky's *The Soldier's Tale*) and 'Sparky's Magic Piano', as well as the piano in *Salad Days* by Julian Slade. There is much more of symbolism in each of these instances than merely drawing attention to the sound of the instrument; there are too many examples of such a sound used primarily for its dramatic impact in opera or programme music – trumpets and horns, tubas and indeed most if not all orchestral instruments have been so used in one work or another – for there to be any doubt about the distinction I seek to draw.

A relevant analogy is the sound of the cock crowing in Rimsky-Korsakov's *Golden Cockerel*. Based on a fairy tale by Pushkin, this opera illustrates lightly and humorously but faithfully a remarkable range of esoteric symbols: a magician, a part sung effectively by a counter-tenor, 'out of this world', as an enlightened guide; duality epitomized in the two identical princes at war with each other to the death; and even (in 1954 at the Royal Opera House, Covent Garden, as produced by Sir Robert Helpmann) a choreographed dance of the chromosomes![10]

In a magical guise a musical instrument, not just music, has been used to depict an influence beyond entertaining, beyond even the invocation of a mood of serenity or exhilaration. In the extraordinary and, far from easy-to-read book, *All and Everything*,[11] the author, Gurdjieff, through the mouth of Beelzebub, a space traveller who makes several visits to this planet, records a conversation with a dervish from Bokhara in Asia, evidently in historical time, about the vibrations of sound. There are descriptions of instruments constructed specially for experiments with aural vibrations, experiments so advanced that a chord may be sounded calculated to bring up a boil on the leg of any mortal – and another to dissipate it; Beelzebub's relative immortality renders him immune and he has problems in explaining this to his dervish friend because of the vow of non-disclosure to any earthling[12] of his alien origin.

If conjurers can perform certain of their most baffling tricks by mirrors, the universe beyond tricks and illusions relies – for all and everything – on vibrations.[13]

---

[1] See *Through Music to the Self*, op.cit. p.119–20.

[2] There is no more fascinating book on the subject of its title than *The Wellsprings of Music* by Curt Sachs (Martinus Nijhoff, The Hague, 1962, and Da Capo Press Inc., New York).

[3] Peter Shaffer's *Amadeus*, suggesting that the Queen of the Night represented Mozart's mother-in-law.

[4] *The Greek Myths*, Penguin Books, 1955, Vol. I, p.77.

[5] ibid., p.81.

[6] Second leader, 18 February 1984.

[7] Letter in *The Times*, 23 February 1984.

[8] Peregrine (Penguin) 1967, p.175.

[9] Included in a selection of Masefield's poems by John Betjeman, Heinemann 1978.

[10] The meticulously regulated movements of chromosomes preparing to divide and then dividing within the ripening ovum, in readiness for possible impregnation and conception. See *The Unknown Spirit* by Jean Charon, Chapter VII (Coventure, 1983).

[11] Routledge & Kegan Paul, 1950, p.880 et seq.

[12] cf. Arthur C. Clarke's sci-fi novel *Childhood's End*, Sidgwick & Jackson, 1964.

[13] For illuminating exposition of the relationship between music and magic see *Through Music to the Self*, op.cit.

6
BLOW BUGLE, BLOW

From Arcadia we must turn to more Martian, martial themes, in which only in recent centuries have unmusical aural vibrations prevailed. As an elephant trumpets in anger, a lion roars and, with a certain voice, a dog barks to scare a stranger or a foe, the canine equivalent of whistling in the dark, so the blood-curdling yell of Pan, or of the wild 'satyr' in the cave-mouth, turned into the first battle cry of tribal warriors, precursors of the gang (as in Bernstein's *West Side Story*).

Later there were songs to sustain flagging spirits, to help the rhythm of marching men too weary consciously to put one foot before the other. 'It's a long way to Tipperary . . .', 'Pack up your troubles in your old kit bag . . .' will have sustained Poor Bloody Infantrymen of the British Army during World War I, marching to mutilation and death in the trenches and over the top and, for any still mobile survivors, back again. In my generation the same songs kept up the spirit of Boy Scouts marching to and from peaceful camp sites. Round the camp fires we sang old songs, mindless of their original associations.

Sense the stark realism of Frederic Manning's poem *Grotesque*:

> These are the damned circles Dante trod,
> Terrible in hopelessness,
> But even skulls have their humour,
> An eyeless and sardonic mockery;

> And we,
> Sitting with streaming eyes in the acrid smoke,
> That murks our foul, damp billet,
> Chant bitterly, with raucous voices
> As a choir of frogs
> In hideous irony, our patriotic songs.

In World War II, in Europe at least, it was considered rather old-fashioned to march. So trivialized was the art of creating rousing or patriotic songs that the hubris of 'Run rabbit, run . . .' and 'Let's hang out our washing on the Siegfried Line . . .' predictably blew back into the faces of those civilians who sang them, inviting nemesis by giving not a thought to the maudlin, boastful sentiment of the 'lyrics' (luckily 'There'll always be an England' and 'The white cliffs of Dover' survived). The serving men, less vainglorious than the silly words implied, sang them but seem to have preferred, across the frontiers, *Lili Marlene*; evidently they would gladly have sat wooing under any tree anywhere – no matter with whose girl – while hopelessly throwing to the girls they left behind the line 'Don't sit under an apple tree with anyone else but me . . .'

Possessiveness and jealousy – its corollary – are emotions provoked by a beloved which are not confined to those on active service. To live in constant terror of death for oneself or for those one loves concentrates wonderfully that part of the mind from which spurts, as if pulsed by the heart, not doggerel but real poetry, like this from Isaac Rosenberg's *Louse Hunting* –

> . . . See the merry limbs in hot Highland fling
> Because some wizard vermin
> Charmed from the quiet this revel
> When our ears were half lulled
> By the dark music
> Blown from Sleep's trumpet.

That dark music has, at one time or another, denied most of us music performed to entertain us which we regard as more real. To my regret, if not shame, I have always dozed through the relatively light, yet heavy music of the first act of Strauss's opera *Der Rosenkavalier*, regarded by many opera-lovers as his greatest. But I awoke to a world of (Western) music in wartime when I was peripatetic in Britain – if I may be allowed to forget the barren hours of *Roll out the Barrel* . . . and its like – and a number of great works I cannot now hear without being transported back automatically and instantly to a barrack room or mess some way from home. These works include notably Sibelius's seventh symphony and Bartok's violin concerto (No. 2), Vaughan Williams' fierce fourth symphony, Stravinsky's *Firebird* suite, Beethoven's *Kreutzer* sonata, his *Archduke* trio and his powerful 32 variations in C minor, Bloch's *Schelomo*, and Elgar's cello concerto played by Casals in Chester Cathedral. All of these were overshadowed by the sound of the *Last Post* blown, on an NCO's course near Uxbridge in November 1940, each night after we had turned in, the first fires of the night's blitz over London raging in the distance to the east.

Without a chance to check, I was told that the *Last Post* included all the army's messages conveyed by bugle call – reveille, 'come to the cook-house door, boys', the advance, the retreat and I know not what others. A lad, Ivin by name I think, was the bugler; he seemed to understand where the last unresolved cadence led. I will not mind if my ashes are scattered to the last notes of that open-ended, questioning, haunting dark music.

In the Second World War, the pervasive tannoy (a loudspeaker system) or the relatively secret, if buggable intercom replaced communication by drum and fife and the bugle or trumpet calls of previous centuries. Song, round the Naafi piano or vicariously blasted from the radio, might still boost morale or, in my case, rather depress it. But nowadays the use of instrumental music to signify and somehow to symbolize patriotic fervour is confined to the ceremonial occasion on the parade-ground. There it is at less risk of being drowned by the cacophony of mechanical weaponry and low-flying jets than it would be on the battleground.

From the earliest experiments in creating percussive sounds and rhythms with different forms of rattles and by hitting objects or striking them together, preferably those with some resonance, the range of moods to be reached and touched off by timbre and beat has been recognized. A sophisticated drum with instantly adjustable pitch is not needed to correspond with or cut across the rhythm of heartbeats under circumstances of relative stress or relaxation. For a forced march to battle, a funeral march, a triumphal march, a march to the scaffold or for a slogging march turning into a rout, the beat of drums can convey and match a mood and vary it incomparably. The complex and ever-changing pulses with which, mostly unaware, we live – telephones, typewriters, time signals, tills, the sirens of ambulances and police cars and burglar alarms are obvious examples – may, with the flow of adrenalin, bring sensitive people near to always amoral hysteria.

Must not the drum's origins lie before those even of the simplest pipe? Yet even the use of drums in highly sophisticated Western music – such as Bartok's sonata for two pianos and percussion or Daniel Jones' sonata for three (otherwise) unaccompanied kettledrums – cannot compete with the subtlety of meaning, the vitality and stamina of drums used among African tribes for communication and to accompany elaborate dances and ceremonies involving highly-charged emotions, or in improvised Indian music, extending far beyond the relative crudity of military usage.

Less universally, musical instruments have been employed for patriotic purposes. While the bagpipe, a very ancient instrument, seems to have originated independently in Hungary and India as well as in Ireland and Northumbria, it has successfully migrated with its pre-eminent reputation from the Scottish Highlands to Ghurka Regiments of the British Army. The penetrating sound emanating from the reed pipe accompanied by a set of drones creates a characteristic atmosphere, at the same time stirring and nostalgic even for those whose native traditions have no known connection with the bagpipe. How much more effective must this eerie and strangely harmonized sound have been on the battlefield for those for whom the bagpipe is, as a national instrument, at once patriotic and sentimental.

Obviously the effectiveness of music in battle must have been judged by the clarity, penetration and distinctiveness of any message to be imparted, its practicality in terms of ready availability (what use the trumpet if no trumpeter survive fit to blow it?), its mobility and, most important, its known or rightly anticipated influence on morale. The message had to be associated in the minds of serving men of the 'home team' with the voice of reliable authority, successful in attack and prudent in retreat, to instil confidence even in the face of the clearest contrary evidence of the senses. If at the same time the enemy were made to feel anxious or confused, awed or terrified, this musical germ became an embryonic weapon in psychological warfare.

That such a use of music is not to be despised even in contemporary wartime conditions is proved by an immediately identifiable group of four notes – 'fate knocking at the door' – from the opening (and/or the scherzo) of Beethoven's fifth symphony. This became the symbol of ultimate victory among the Allied Nations in World War II. In morse code three dots and a dash represent the letter 'V' hence 'V for Victory'. As a signature tune for Allied broadcasts to the mainland of Europe, fettered by Nazi forces, it was magnificent. It embodied an increasingly reassuring undertone as the grim struggle entered into its final phases. Whether it had, in the same instant, the opposite effect on the morale of German serving men and women and civilians is less certain, but those who heard it surely did not miss the irony of the Allied choice of a tune from the music of a German!

Music, often the same music, e.g. *Lili Marlene*, is performed to sustain the morale of opposing forces. In his 'Study in Religion and Politics', *Grey Eminence*,[2] Aldous Huxley described how Father Joseph, Cardinal Richelieu's 'grey eminence', recruited his Calvarian nuns – 'communities of cloistered contemplatives' – during the siege of La Rochelle in the course of the Thirty Years War, as 'powerful praying machines, capable, if put into high gear and worked for twenty-four hours a day, seven days a week, of precipitating, so to speak, out of the ether, very considerable quantities of divine favour'. Sometimes the energies of these nuns in prayer resulted in success and sometimes in failure. The besieged Protestants in La Rochelle were dying of starvation, 'but faith in their Calvinist God and the hope of English succour made them deaf to all talk of surrender'. Aldous Huxley writes scathingly about the nature of petitionary prayer, in this instance of the Calvinists in conflict with the Calvarians like Tweedle Dum and Tweedle Dee. The influence of music, whoever may hear it in wartime, may be distinguished from such blasphemy, such a mis-understanding and misuse of the object and power of prayer, such an abuse of faith.

Listening to music may, effortlessly, like sleep, recharge run-down 'batteries'. Prayer is at the same time a vastly more complex and infinitely simpler operation; it requires a special kind of effort which might be called inverse. 'Self-denial' has become associated, as a watchword of the Salvation Army, with a certain worldly unselfishness, not to be denigrated but not at all what the expression might otherwise have been understood to mean. 'Self-remembering' is liable to be misunderstood by those who strive for 'God-remembering' or who distinguish to watch and to pray as two functions. To watch and to recollect are essential parts of the process of praying meaningfully; everyone who prays from the heart will discover the melting of contradictions, the positive wonder of a state of release; I and thou a binary system.

> *Free Rain*[3]
> Can ever again
> Rain
> Drop, since Portia observed
> It 'droppeth', gentle?
> Gentle, never but it pours,
> Pours then, but gentle.
> Free
> It is, like all the best things
> In life – space, colours,
> Top-soil, air, sunlight,
> Soft sounds, silence,
> Tenderness, the quality of mercy,
> Night.
> All good things
> Must end, only the best
> Good enough for you: may you be served
> Right.
> Lord have mercy
> On me . . .

Music seems to mediate between warring elements in one's own being, elements not at ease with each other, elements torn by contradictions, distressed by the tensions between and the irresolution of hopes and fears. One friend said to me that when she is upset she turns to Brahms to calm and console her; another independently named Brahms as a composer whose music she especially loved – but not to listen to when she was distressed in any way.

Such conflicting views cannot be understood in isolation. They may be generalizations, even for those two friends who spoke to me with assurance as if recalling specific occasions or moods. Extrapolations from particular but isolated experiences, may, in practice, be not generally applicable even for the individuals concerned. Why did I not think to ask questions from which I might have judged whether being upset for one is materially similar to being distressed for the other? Did they both mean *any* Brahms? Or else, which Brahms?

In the terror, anxiety and boredom of war, those who find nourishment in 'great' music seldom have any choice of listening. All of them will be likely to ⸴ ⸴preciate any such music which they may be fortunate enough to hear. When on leave I was able to attend a number of the war-time lunch-hour concerts at the National Gallery for which the pianist Myra Hess was honoured with a DBE, as a great musician as well as for her initiative, perseverance and courage in organizing those particular concerts. Each month one superb painting from the National Gallery's collection was brought from the security of a Welsh mine, a cave in the Chilterns or wherever it was stored away from the bombing, to take its chance of destruction in Trafalgar Square. To the right of the main entrance, in a gallery with bare walls, there would be a daily concert for all who cared and were free to come. From the scant record of my contemporary diaries I see that the concerts I attended between July 1941 and April 1943 included those given by the Blech String Quartet, Denis Matthews and Harry Blech, Eda Kersey and Kathleen Long, Max Rostal and Maria Lidka, Isolde Menges and Eileen Joyce, the 'RAF Strings', Dame Myra Hess and Irene Scharrer and finally Benno Moisewitch and Jan Van Der Gucht.

Did any music-lovers, I wonder, ever turn away because the music of the day was by some composer, Brahms perhaps, whose music was known to exacerbate a bad mood – and they were in such a mood that day? I can only usefully ask for myself and cannot, for lack of information, answer for anyone else. And for lack of information I cannot answer for myself either. I am quite sure that I went, whatever the programme, whenever I could to those concerts: and was duly uplifted. That subsequently I might deliberately have avoided a concert at which a Bruckner symphony was to be performed tells me nothing about the Michael Rubinstein of 1941 who had never heard of Bruckner let alone heard any of his symphonies. And if he had had the opportunity, might not his relative starvation for 'good music' have driven him even to a Bruckner concert *faute de mieux*?

The solace and the boost to the spirits of music in wartime is magnified by deprivation and bleak contrasts. This must be true, of course, for those on each side of the conflict. Apart from the urge to win, or to lose quickly if only that would end the horror of it, anyone can recognize the mixture of good and bad in the helpless human beings on both sides of any war. Where 'kill or be killed' is the law of the civilized jungle of modern warfare, what relevance have 'good' and 'bad'? Significant relevance just the same. The practical recognition of common humanity may be found anywhere and is of the same quality wherever it survives brutalization. And even where it does not, music resembles the quality of mercy still. Musicians in the concentration camp at Auschwitz were preserved from annihilation in the gas chambers in order to accompany with sublime music the last herding of the victims; and to console their tormentors and executioners too.[4] I am unable to comment on the irony of that.

---

[1] Frederic Manning, *Eidolon*, Murray, 1917, quoted from Jon Silkin's anthology *First World War Poetry*, Penguin, 1979.

[2] Chatto & Windus, 1941.

[3] The author, 1976 (unpublished).

[4] *The Musicians of Auschwitz* by Fania Fenelon, Michael Joseph, 1977. Those who have been spared the trauma of witnessing the agony of others may find a contemplation of Titian's most curious late masterpiece, *The Flaying of Marsyas*, illuminating. In other paintings of the same story, such as the two canvases by Jacopo Plama (1544–1628) in the Hertzon Anton Urich Musem, Brunswick, entitled *Apollo and Marsyas*, and Ribera's *The Flaying of Marsyas* (1630 – one of two versions, in the Musée Nationale de Capodimonte, Brussels) the agony of Marsyas is depicted as if the object of the artists was to feed a hunger for scenes of cruelty, presaging the current vogue for horror comics and video nasties. But Titian's illustration of the myth (see illustration) does not come into this category: Titian's Marsyas seems to bear his flaying with detached stoicism, as if he recognizes that it is a desirable cathartic operation rather than a capriciously determined slow torture. Marsyas is here depicted as an accident-prone victim of fate. Around him are relatively disinterested figures: there is no sadistic expression on the faces of the two men tearing the skin from Marsyas's body nor any expression of agonized compassion on the face of the satyr coming from behind him, carrying a bucket. The Rodin-like thinker coolly watching a small dog lapping up blood from a pool below the hanging body shows no care for the suffering individual, while a small satyr-child is only concerned to feign an effort to restrain a large dog, salivating in anticipation of a meaty meal. To one side, gazing upwards ecstatically, Apollo fiddles away (but as if handling a viol for the first time, experimentally). In the centre Marsyas himself hangs upside down from a tree, as if posing for the Major Arcana Tarot card *The Hanging Man*. What *is* going on? A psycho-spiritual drama of whose symbolic validity even Titian may not have been consciously aware.

7

MUSIC MOVES

Berlioz' 'March to the Scaffold', in his *Symphonie Fantastique* may be recognized as one kind of Danse Macabre in the context of a programme. While dancing may be a free activity it has historically been more often formalized in association with an established musical form – a minuet, a polonaise or a Scottish reel in the West, for example – or the subject of choreographic treatment. Music is, of course, not essential for dancing. But given the opportunity, even encouraged if at first shy in company many people may more easily express their feelings spontaneously through movement than through words or song. Perhaps 'dance music' is a tautology.

Before the 1914–18 war the Swiss Emile Jaques-Dalcroze (1865–1950) invented a system known as 'eurhythmics' whereby bodily movement expressed a response to rhythm in music – the subject of consideration in Chapter 13.

Insofar as music involves essentially a rhythmic element it may stimulate a dancing feeling even if that is not translated into an actual dance movement. Such a movement may include the automatic tendency to tap a toe in time with music of regular or syncopated beat or whose rhythmic aberrations may be anticipated; or, to the irritation of neighbours at a concert, to beat time, more or less, as an incompetent conductor might.

It is surely no coincidence that the instrumental sonata, which in the case of a sonata for orchestra is known as a symphony, was developed from about the middle of the eighteenth century from the earlier suites which included such dance forms as the allemande, courante, sarabande, minuet and gigue (or jig – like others derived from earlier peasant or folk dances). The elaboration of sonata-form, in particular but not exclusively for first movements, involves key modulations which render its use for atonal music inappropriate. Haydn and Mozart retained the minuet, generally as a third movement following a relatively slow second movement, for their works in sonata form. Beethoven, following Haydn, ultimately substituted substance and structure in lively, sometimes diabolic scherzos which evolved from the minuets.

'I got rhythm! I got music!' went a popular song of the 1920s charleston era. It was right. A proportion of the population may be tone-deaf as others are colour-blind but everyone's got rhythm – a factor fundamental to the therapeutic use of music.

Little wonder therefore that works as disparate as Beethoven's late piano sonata in B flat Op.106 (the *Hammerklavier*) and Mahler's symphonic song-cycle *The Song of the Earth* for mezzo-soprano, tenor and orchestra have been choreographed and used to accompany dancing in the classic ballet repertoire of the Royal Ballet Company, Covent Garden. The *Hammerklavier* is Beethoven's longest piano sonata and seems to me his most emotionally complex work for solo piano. Mahler tried to embody in *The Song of the Earth* as in some, perhaps all, of his numbered symphonies, an all-embracing view of the world. Yet these huge works were chosen as the musical settings for ballets when it had been fashionable no longer to base ballets on music specially written for and often commissioned by choreographers and impresarios following the example of Diaghilev.

It is idle to pretend that there is a category of 'music written only to be listened to'. For a dedicated composer there is of course 'music that must be composed' and its performance and appreciation by an audience, let alone its commercial success, may be of lesser significance. Many great composers, from Haydn, Mozart and Beethoven to Bartok (*Mikrokosmos* for piano and his 44 duos, for violin) have written works specifically for their pupils, or for performance by their patrons and other musicians whose technique had not reached a professional standard; that many such works give pleasure is a bonus. But the majority of works by professional composers are obviously intended for wider audiences. The test is whether in performance their qualities justify inclusion in concert or radio programmes and, eventually, in record catalogues.

Walt Disney used certain classical works in his *Fantasia*, a programme of colour cartoon films which included, in my view regrettably, Beethoven's *Pastoral* symphony. When I now listen to that work I am haunted by those ghastly galloping centaurs, so that Beethoven's 'Recollections of Country Life' (Expression of Emotion rather than Painting) is converted into a literal and grotesque visualization. Another item was based on a version of the splendid toccata and fugue in D minor long attributed to Bach as written for the organ, in a version orchestrated by Leopold Stokowski who conducted the programme; for this Disney's cartoon was appropriately abstract. Did it enhance the music? It provided the visual element of a non-human and non-anthropomorphic ballet. For those who would not have chosen to listen to the work at all or who, having done so, would have failed to come to terms with its non-programmatic idiom the imagery of the film may have provided just that connecting link with its dancing rhythms to render it not only palatable but actually comprehensible and even pleasurable. Peter Williams has more recently argued convincingly[1] that the work was more likely composed by someone in the mid-nineteenth century than by or transcribed by Bach, and not written for the organ but for the solo violin!

The visual factor seems to me to be a specific attraction in concert-going. A pianist's fingers may be said, colloquially, to dance over the keys. A conductor may mesmerize an audience by charisma and hold its attention by semi-balletic, individualistic movements. Many soloists develop idiosyncrasies whose musical significance may or may not be apparent but which are nevertheless, if not mere affectations copied perhaps from a teacher, the expressions in physical form of those inner reactions which accompany the experience of the complex of emotions represented by the music or at least the performer's interpretation of it. How could it be otherwise when rhythm integral to a composition's melody, harmony, instrumentation and form must stimulate those parts of the mind sensitive to movement and, for players and listeners alike, invoke a dancing feeling.

The whole man may participate in an orchestral performance

experienced at a concert in a manner not possible in listening to a live radio or even a television broadcast. The orchestra as well as the conductor is performing a kind of ballet. In a work such as Bartok's sonata for two pianists and two necessarily highly proficient percussionists, a performance can be a thrilling visual experience *almost* irrespective of the exceptional merits of the music itself.

An extra-musical pleasure can be derived from watching music being performed, just as it can for the performers from the physical act of playing. Music may also evoke pleasure of different kinds for the listener. Admiration for the subtle synchronization of the performers is often an important contributory factor to applause. There is tension from the recognition of better than merely professional co-ordination and admiration is akin, in part, to that accorded the training and team-work of the *corps de ballet* of a great company, or a polished team of gymnasts. The sight of the precision of players 'entering' may draw attention to the sounds they produce, generally missed in a performance which is only heard. For some, a similar advantage is conferred by following the score, no less valuable at home than in a concert hall. In either case the visual element may enable the music to be followed to help concentration. At a concert tension or tedium is relieved by the physical action of applauding and there is pleasure to be derived also from its anticipation. It is as well to beware of the risk that the sight of physical activity or the following of a score may distract from the real or purported objective – to *listen* with attention.

However this analysis of the contribution of visual aids to the appreciation of music is superficial if it does not lead to the consideration of other possible subjective effects on the listener. The experience of movement itself, through the senses of hearing, sight and an inner sense of rhythm, should not be decried. It is not only the lonely and isolated for whom the sensation of activity, as conveyed in music, may be subliminally attractive. That sensation stimulates those parts of the mind which function in connection with some aspect of movement, though differently according to the individual's balance of mind-functions. Hence one listener may be content with the endless rhythmic flow of whatever dance music is fashionable – the 'pops'. Another may, perhaps surprisingly, never tire of Viennese waltzes or Tchaikovsky's music famous in classical ballet – *Swan Lake* and the *Nutcracker Suite*. For those of more sophisticated musical taste an unavoidable indulgence in popular works may be a form of mental cruelty. Such music, lacking variety plays on too restricted or familiar a complex of emotions. Torture, then, is not too strong a word! And, for those with a less cultivated taste, it seems that more complex music may be no less painfully boring and disagreeable.

What then are the processes whereby the same music may be blissful for some and agonizing for others? It seems that the subconscious sympathy of the listener for the representation of a particular complex of emotions (to use yet again that invaluable expression of Deryck Cooke's) embodied by the composer in a particular musical work, will dictate his inner reactions to it – not necessarily the same at every hearing. For instance, an emotional-intellectual part of his mind may enable him to concentrate on the form of the music throughout, especially if he is relatively familiar with it in the case of music of any formal complexity. But some private problem or worry may occasionally or constantly break such concentration. Or a listener who is given to blanket day-dreaming may find one work or another, or some particular style of work agreeably stimulating to the undirected imagination. At concerts the sight of other members of the audience may be as attractive to the attention – literally as well as metaphorically – as the performers themselves; then the music itself is likely to be irrelevant rather than distractive!

A computer is not required to calculate what combination of factors will render one concert programme or series more commercially successful than another. The big names, artists with style and charisma, stars built up by impresarios, managers and publicity agents and to a lesser but not negligible extent by the reviews of music critics, will fill concert halls – but the stars may price themselves out of particular markets. Then the impresarios see and seize the opportunity to introduce promising tyros, the next generation of masters, preferably with success in international competition to commend them in advance.

What has this 'star quality' to do with the appreciation of music as distinct from essential commercial viability? For a successful career in music a soloist or conductor requires exceptional drive, stamina and tenacity. A reliable, even phenomenal technique must be acquired and maintained. Outside the profession it is hard to appreciate the application, self-discipline and ambition essential if talent is to be nurtured, developed and projected. And all of these for any who deserve to succeed at the top of the profession should go for nothing without innate musicality.

A wide range of interpretation of musical works of any merit can extend a listener's insight into and appreciation of those works. An interpretation may be found unacceptable if one cannot rely on the integrity of the interpreter. His integrity is compounded of his technique at the service of his musicality and his musicality may fairly be judged by the sense of satisfaction or satisfying provocation invoked in the listener. I derive the desirable sense of satisfaction from a feeling that the complex of emotions the composer embodied in the work has been faithfully reproduced through a corresponding complex of emotions of the performer. A performance may demonstrate technical mastery but at the same time illustrate a lack of integrity on the part of the performer. Typically this is evident where the performer introduces an element of showmanship inconsistent with the composer's overall complex of emotions in the piece; in that sense a performer may fail convincingly to reproduce the composer's own musical integrity.

Many audiences, however, may be attracted by and appreciative of a kind of showmanship, appropriate only in works for virtuosos and unacceptable to those who might claim to be 'more musical'. So be it! I see as *an* object of performance the satisfaction of audiences. If some are satisfied by or actually prefer performances which I would, from the point of view of musicality, regard as meretricious rather than meritorious, I would not wish to see them deprived of their pleasure. How else than by experiencing a wide range of performances and by appraising them might the musical discrimination of such audiences be developed. Discrimination, like taste, can best be acquired through comparison enhanced by guidance. With discrimination comes a new kind of satisfaction in any given musical performance. Satisfaction need not be complete – indeed complete satisfaction in this context is rare indeed, since no complex of emotions (which is what we are still considering) of a composer, performer or listener, can itself be 'complete'. To be 'complete' it would have to be 'perfect' – for man *almost* an impossibility *almost* by definition! – save in the somewhat esoteric sense that one's Being attracts one's life[2] or that we create our lives, so that what occurs is inevitable and so, existentially, is perfect.

In commercial terms it may be that the pull of at least one great name

– a famous soloist appearing with a relatively unknown conductor, or *vice versa* – is more important than a well-constructed programme. There has always been the moan from those concerned in promoting unknown or less popular works, that to fill a concert hall yet again with an all -Tchaikovsky or -Beethoven programme is not only ultimately self-defeating from the point of view of audience-building but must also tend to produce hackneyed performances by bored orchestras – bored, it may be, by their conductors' apathy rather than by the music they are asked to play. There is some truth in both contra-indications.

Nevertheless the problems faced by those whose task it is to construct programmes which are musically justified, attractive *and* commercially viable is bedevilled by factors extraneous to audience satisfaction. A list of only some of these factors will illustrate the nature and complexity of the task. Confining ourselves for this purpose to London-based orchestras, it must be borne in mind that they are dependent on subsidies from the Arts Council, the BBC or the municipality and probably from commercial or industrial sponsors too; they could not exist from ticket sales alone. Then the availability on each convenient date of a suitable concert-hall must be matched with touring, festival and recording commitments when the programme for a concert or a season of concerts is being planned – one to three years in advance. The programmes for concerts given by other, perhaps visiting orchestras at about the same time must be taken into consideration to avoid the risk of splitting an assumed audience for any particular occasion.

A programme may be built round a soloist who is a guaranteed box-office draw. Then, if blessed with almost super-human stamina, he or she may be expected to perform in two or, rarely these days, three major concertos at the same concert. The availability of a particular soloist and conductor as well as a hall may, in practice, dictate one or more of the major items in the programme. Within a given season there are likely to be several 'themes' – centenary celebrations or a concentration on one composer, performer or era, but a very limited number, involving, again, the prospect of clashes to be avoided.

These are not the only factors with which the concert promoter must juggle a year or two in advance. He must also consider the aggregate length of the works in each half of a concert, possible timing for broadcasting and the desirability of including an unusual work which will be well rehearsed for recording purposes just before the projected date of the concert. There might be a tendency to overlook the musical taste of members of the prospective audience were its commercial relevance not so significant. Even if subsidies were guaranteed irrespective of the audiences attracted to concerts over a season, it is harmfully disheartening for orchestras and soloists to play to small audiences, however appreciative. A small audience cannot adequately convey appreciation in a large hall.

Londoners are of course exceptionally fortunate in the daily choice of public music-making – three opera houses, two of them with first-class 'resident' companies (operas sometimes alternating with ballets), the Royal Albert Hall where most of the seats are no longer affected by utterly deplorable acoustics, the Royal Festival Hall, Queen Elizabeth Hall and Purcell Room, the Barbican and the old Wigmore Hall. Other halls are suitable for irregular use, for contemporary music and other enterprising music-making. The huge population of Greater London and the immense turnover of visitors should indeed simplify the task of musically sound and commercially successful programme-building in London.

There remains the risk, in less expansively endowed provincial areas, of a satiated, blasé audience. Outside London in places where a concert is an occasional event, an ambitious programme which might deter regular concert-goers in the metropolis, can attract a full audience. The risk of any clash of programmes may more easily be avoided; but there the overall choice is inevitably much restricted compared with the London scene, endowed with so many people in search of entertainment and an artistically stimulating experience.

In a culture such as ours, for most concert-goers a desire to hear a particular work performed is likely to be a rare factor in deciding to attend a concert or in choosing which concert to attend. Almost any concert may be seen as an opportunity to share an experience with a chosen companion which can be expected to give pleasure to both: then the choice of the companion and his or her convenience may be more significant than the music to be shared, or its performers. Perhaps some music or some performers may be ruled out in any event, as a result of previous experience or of hearsay; alternatively a policy of experimentation may be preferred.

The mood, the complex of emotions, likely to be evoked by a particular work or programme or series of concerts may, then, be the factor least relevant to a concert-goer's choice, whether it be made days or weeks in advance or spontaneously at the last moment. It should not on this account be dismissed as irrelevant. Trends and fashions in concert-going will reflect not just the temporary bias of concert-promoters who manipulate the preferences of the audiences they seek to attract. There will be underlying factors, awaiting investigation and analysis by social scientists and anthropologists, which render potential audiences more or less amenable at different periods to music corresponding in a general way to a particular range of complexes of emotion. Programmes of music may therefore be constructed with a view to satisfying such moods.

In this context two further passages from *The Language of Music* make relevant points:

What exactly is meant by 'feeling the emotion in the music', or more precisely, 'transforming the heard sound of the music into emotional experience'? How does this process actually work? We must suppose that, in the unconscious of the musical listener, professional or layman, a state of affairs exists, musically speaking, similar to that which exists in the unconscious of the composer. In other words, there will be similar groups of memories of the expressive uses of the various tonal tensions, attached to non-musical experiences of a similar nature; and the same subdivision into groups of memories of the various melodic uses of these tensions . . .[3]

It should be clear by now that to say that a composer writes music out of his whole experience is not to entertain crude notions of music's dependency on life – to imagine, say, that the melancholy of the Fortieth Symphony was the immediate result of an influx of bills into the poverty-stricken composer's home, or that the comparative joy of the *Jupiter* arose out of the receipt of a large loan from a friend. An artist's emotions are not the playthings of trivial events, being rooted in his unconscious, where they form his basic life-attitudes; the Fortieth Symphony and the *Jupiter* are visions of the sadness and the joy of life respectively, as experienced by Mozart – not in his superficial, everyday reactions, but in his deep, enduring self.[4]

When the available range of Western 'serious' music of the last four hundred years or so has been sampled by a 'serious' listener over a period of just a few years he will find, according to his own non-musical

73

emotional experiences, his own affinity for certain composers and so his preferences. A listener's emotions need, no more than an artist's, be 'the playthings of trivial events'. Therefore it is of little significance that his choice of concert performance to attend may have to be made weeks beforehand; or that at any particular time a radio programme presents an opportunity rather than a choice more sensitive than the crude 'on' or 'off'. That sort of choice may be dictated more often by external convenience or the occasion, than by the actual music to be broadcast. A progression from 'yes' or 'no' to 'this' not 'that' is significant evidence of a maturing discrimination.

---

[1] Radio 3, 10 June 1981.
[2] Gurdjieff.
[3] Deryck Cooke, op.cit p.206.
[4] ibid. p.235.

8

MUSIC AS A TOOL

Dancing is an expression of emotions. These emotions may be either experienced at the time or simulated, based on a recollection of emotions previously experienced. Dancing does not require the accompaniment of music any more than music, however the rhythm may be emphasized, demands the accompaniment of actual dancing.

It is possible that in some prehistoric groupings of mankind two million or so years ago, a form of singing or music-making preceded speech or constituted part of it; or *was* a form of speech. That is what it probably is in the case of some species of whales, and in birds who may revel in communication and be quite ignorant of the music they make incidentally – in which we revel. However, so far as linguistic anthropologists can judge at present, communication in relation to movement, to *our* physical functioning, was probably of great significance for aeons before the urge came into existence to communicate emotions otherwise than physically.

In the ape house at a zoo some animals repeat characteristic noise patterns whose significance is not unlike a simplification of Deryck Cooke's 'basic terms'. These may sound roughly or vaguely musical. In the same way the language of the 'stone age' tribe investigated by the anthropologists H.J. Heinz and Marshall Lee[1] involved whistling sounds too subtle for a civilized Westerner to employ. As Deryck Cooke points out,[2] the wailing of the Simpleton in Mussorgsky's opera

Boris Godunov is 'taken up as an ostinato for his lament over the future fate of Russia' – a highly sophisticated theme for a Simpleton; and Cooke gives numerous examples to support that wailing phrase as one of his 'basic terms'. This is onomatopoeia in reverse; in the choice of sounds, rather than words, to fit the 'sense' of an emotional experience, or meaning to be conveyed. A baby howls in a particular way, drawing attention to a state of distress; an adult will more likely speak or shout with a similar aim. But that basic musical, non-verbal howl is more deeply expressive, like an aural archetypal symbol.[3]

Deryck Cooke postulated, not very convincingly, sixteen basic terms to express a variety of powerful emotions within a scale from supreme joy to anguished grief. In some instances they seem to overlap. I am interested in a range which may be regarded as simpler, less subtle and so, in a sense, *more* basic. It would include happiness (which Scriabin would extend to ecstasy), misery, fear, anger, threatening, cajoling, soothing (a lullaby), encouraging (suitable for a University of the Air signature tune), loving and hating – the most commonly experienced emotions of mankind for hundreds of thousands of years.

These emotions have within the period accessible to historical assessment been projected by music among people of the widest range of cultural maturation. Music has been used for the direct communication of emotions as distinct from its ability to enable us to reflect on or to recall them. Composers re-activate in their works the most subtle and complex emotional experiences. César Franck's only string quartet, composed in 1889, exemplifies the re-use of themes, from one movement to another (in reverse order in the last movement) rather than the development of themes, 'for development could easily confuse the identity of themes so closely related'.[4] Listeners in turn, and passively may imagine that they are reminded of such experiences of the composers, but essentially *use* music as a reminder of their own recollection of their own experiences, though seldom for the purpose of renewing, reliving the experience itself. The difference is so obvious that it is not noticed. In this context music is not even recognized for what it is: a tool, not just a diversion.

Music as an archetypal remembrancer, music as a diversion or distraction, music as a tool . . . Of course the three categories of 'use' overlap. But in taking the sound of music for granted in modern life and, in the thrall of the ubiquitous 'personal hi-fi', its uses are mostly disregarded or neglected. That music as diversion or distraction seems to have overtaken its use as a tool, available for some extra-aural purpose, is one side of a coin; on the other may be found evidence of a sociological revolution, itself of cultural significance and so of anthropological interest.

It must be difficult for those born since, say, 1940 to realize the nature of the aural revolution effected by the radio since the ending of the Second World War. Before 1940 the wireless had increasingly carried programmes of music of all kinds for listeners in the British Isles but their impact was minimal on the life of any section or grouping of the population; and I have no reason to think it would be otherwise anywhere else in the world. There were programmes of 'serious' music, mostly orchestral, broadcast by the BBC daily, but a music lover in employment would have had to make music himself, or play gramophone records – always a laborious business for any work of more than nine minutes' duration, in those days of 78s whose average playing time was less than four and a half each side. It was no less laborious, but seemed less musically disruptive, to play dance music or jazz on 78s. The radio and the gramophone in these circumstances were of no real significance in relation to the traditional uses of music as tool. Some of these uses are worth assessing before we consider the effects of the post-war aural revolution.

It is arguable that a musical skill itself, like a musical instrument, is widely used as a tool to entertain generally and to encourage conviviality. The individual player, the ensemble creating a corporate pleasure as a team, and the audience are the beneficiaries. A mood may be induced for all present, according to the occasion, that is (in Sufi terms) the time, the place and the company. Mood, then, is part of any message conveyed through music.

In the case of national anthems a mood of patriotic fervour or of complacency may be the message. After the anthem itself is chosen, the emotional atmosphere created by the tune may in the light of subsequent events no longer meet the needs or attitudes of mind of the populace. *God Save the Queen*, which came into use in the mid-eighteenth century, is a splendid tune, as easy to remember and easier to sing than *Pop Goes the Weasel*, the only other tune which, traditionally, the British are supposed to be able to recognize. The second verse is rightly suppressed these days being so bellicose that it hardly appeals even to those who remain royalist in persuasion in the United Kingdom of Great Britain and Northern Ireland. Zealous republicans, however, who may regard themselves as no less patriotic than royalists but happen to have no 'Protector over the water' to drink to in secret, must find anathema the first and third verses; anyway, the rather repetitious third verse is now much less frequently sung or performed than it was, immediately after the first verse, a very few decades ago. In the early 1830s this excellent tune was set to new words in the USA as 'My Country, 'tis of Thee . . .' The tune itself is staunch, rather than bombastic, pompous rather than stirring like *La Marseillaise* (1792) – though that has its argumentative, slightly unsure passage.

As Deryck Cooke observes[5] the Israeli national anthem used 'a stern variant' of the theme of the minor version of *Baa-baa, Black Sheep*, a folk-song common to many countries. The most popular of Smetana's cycle of six symphonic poems, *Ma Vlast* ('My Country' – again!), depicts the river Vltava to evoke, as Cooke says, 'the heroic-tragic past of his native land'. This is a very slightly different version of *Baa-baa, Black Sheep* in which although 'to some extent the theme is infused with a legendary-heroic character, the general effect is not in any way tragic in feeling (rather genial in fact), owing to the buoyant rhythm . . .' That would hardly be suitable, one might think, for Czechoslovakia today.

But does the Israeli national anthem still represent the mood of the Israeli nation? The insistent note of self-pity is characteristic of much Jewish music and no doubt derived from a reaction to the horror of pogroms over centuries in the Diaspora. Might it not be inappropriate as a mood inducer for the contemporary people of Israel? A tragic sense of the past may have been a resilient spring-board for those who traditionally 'remember Jerusalem'; but its constant recall in musical terms may inhibit reminders of other attitudes and sentiments for which a musical equivalent might be chosen, more relevant to problems now faced by Israel and Israelis.

'Pop' music, the music of fashion for the people, can supply 'instant correspondence' in a changing scene. A nation's need for a national anthem – not just any but the 'right' tune for its mood and aspirations – changes while the anthem generally remains, in the absence of a revolution, inviolate for centuries; is this a use or a misuse of music?

Most nations with a national anthem have also another song or two to represent different facets of their outlooks on life. The USA has

The Stars and Stripes and, for less official but no less chauvinistic occasions, 'My Country, 'tis of Thee . . .' Our equivalent to *La Marseillaise* is both *Jerusalem* (as set to music by Parry), for so many years especially invigorating at the last night of the Proms, and *Rule Britannia* (borrowed from the masque, *Alfred*, by Thomas Arne). Both republicans and royalists with only truly patriotic aspirations in mind can sing the words of Blake's poem with equal sincerity – or, cynicism. The recognition of Jerusalem as a symbol, and the urge to fight for it, metaphorically, in every land, might seem desirable in principle, but it could hardly resolve a source of conflict between Arabs and Jews about the city itself. The tensions evoked by Jerusalem the city are not metaphoric and the adoption of the Blake/Parry hymn by the United Nations, with but slight verbal adaptation here and there, could not be relied upon to increase euphony, let alone unity among all its population.

It might be no bad thing, however, to encourage a little national self-analysis, to help each nation to 'Know Itself' first by recalling the historical context of the choice or composition of its national anthem and then by examining the words as well as the tunes which still present its image to the world. To a degree the peoples of every nation traditionally regard their own country as the 'best', the greatest, the most admirable. The claim must be ludicrous of course – only less so than a claim that any single religion is 'the only true religion'. That we cannot see the faults in ourselves though perceiving the same faults and being irritated by them in others is an age-old psychological curiosity. Hence the national anthem sung with conviction and taken for granted as 'right' is probably a more accurate representation of a nation's outlook than its patriots realize. No single anthem can represent the main subtleties and crudities of any nation; or perhaps we can rely on natural forces to ensure that due representation is already achieved, without need for national-analysis.

On a less exalted scale there is music for particular occasions which may convey, like a national anthem, some obvious and some devious messages to those receivers equipped with an appropriate psychological unscrambler. What is one to make, for example, of *Land of Hope and Glory* at Wembley Cup Finals? Elgar's setting of part of his first *Pomp and Circumstance March* in his *Coronation Ode*, to words of A.C. Benson, while appearing to convey only unexceptional cliché-sentiments, introduces two weasel words – 'hope' and 'glory' – just where their relevance to the game of football is at once apt and (unintentionally) snide. Regiments and schools and sporting clubs have their marches and their songs which unconsciously underline the irony of pride in one's image. The banality of the music generally matches the triteness of the words – no doubt nowadays graced with the label 'lyrics' as a reminder that poetry set to music played on the lyre should be regarded as emotional and very personal to the singer.

Across the barriers of nation, class and race, religions have evoked some of the greatest and some of the most trivial music. In the West the Roman Catholic Mass has inspired from many composers, some of them notably not members of the Church of Rome, musical settings of especial grandeur compounded of power and beauty. The Bible has been no less a source of inspiration for many fine oratorios, operas, symphonies and song-cycles. The Judeo-Christian ethic and religio-historic base has permeated the music of our civilization since the Dark Ages so effectively that the music it inspired is no less appreciated, albeit differently, in our largely secular society today than it was when composer, patron, celebrant and congregation assembled to hear the first performance of a Monteverdi madrigal to sacred text or of Haydn's *The Seven Last Words of Our Saviour on the Cross*. Visualize, for further example, the change of perspective over the years for the original 'audiences' compared with almost any contemporary audience towards any of the Masses of Bach, Haydn, Mozart or Schubert, Beethoven's *Missa Solemnis*, Brahms' *German Requiem* and Verdi's *Requiem*; Berlioz' oratorio *The Childhood of Christ* (1854); or Messiaen's *Visions of the Amen* for two pianos or *Twenty Observations of the Child Jesus* for one. British composers of this century have both maintained and enhanced the tradition: Elgar's oratorios *The Apostles* and *The Kingdom* and, to words by Cardinal Newman, *The Dream of Gerontius* preceded Walton's *Belshazzar's Feast*, a setting of Osbert Sitwell's arrangement of words chiefly from the Bible which has in turn been followed by Vaughan Williams, Rubbra, Britten, Tippett and Tavener (born 1944), to name but a few.

Religion was of course a most significant force in the history of Western classical music, and it still is. At the same time music served and still serves the objects of religious assembly and worship. Neither is unthinkable without the other – there is no reason why someone who is tone-deaf should not be as devout as a church organist. Nor why an atheist should not compose, or appreciate and enjoy a performance of a sacred musical work which inspires a spirit of worship in a believer. How then has music been 'used' for religious purposes?

Certainly music in connection with religious services has been attractive as sheer entertainment – especially, as my friend the clergyman pointed out, before music became as intrusive as air in every home. Some would be attracted for purely musical reasons and others for the added pleasure of participation, thus helping to swell congregations and at the same time making church-going itself a delight as well as an assumed duty. For those puritans for whom it was obligatory for reasons of tradition or prestige, any enjoyment which might have been derived from the music would no doubt be rejected and denied. On the lay principle that only foul-tasting medicine can be good for the patient, less than enjoyable church-going should be good for the sinner, or at least for his soul.

It cannot be too fanciful (though unsupported statistically, of course) to suppose that some who came only to appreciate the music stayed to worship. So far as I am aware there is no record either of the converse and no less interesting supposition – that many of those who attended church originally to worship returned primarily to hear and participate in the music.

Over forty years ago I was staying with a French family ostensibly to learn the language, at Enghiens-les-Bains, a sleepy spa near Paris. They introduced me to a charming neighbour, a Jewish Frenchwoman, Madame Neu, who let me strum on a huge harmonium formerly owned by César Franck, while she pumped the bellows if I wanted to play on the pedal keyboard. She herself played the organ at a local synagogue for the Sabbath services on Saturdays and at the church on Sundays; I fancy that was her form of worship – a service to music as a tool of worship by others, no matter what their religion or denomination. Such an ecumenical spirit should be read into my references to church and church-going in this chapter.

Now, without fear of demeaning themselves, some churches employ supposedly popular, though not necessarily 'pop', music to attract young people who will, they hope, stay and return to worship. Nuns practise and perform with guitars, church halls and even churches are occasionally used for pop concerts and discos, as a change from the nowadays accepted function as settings for classical – if not too profane – as well as sacred music.

In most solemn worship Christians kneel, Jews stand. Marked

changes of posture during the service are devised to keep one from dozing off – a risk preserved, in any creed or denomination, for the sermon. And hymns, chants or anthems, for which the whole congregation stands, conveniently serve the same purpose: a secondary use of music, perhaps, but not negligible.

When a congregation joins in the musical interludes, a special sense of unity is experienced, just as it should be in responses and prayers not set to music. This sense of unity is, however, not *the* object of the religious service but it may be *an* object. The experience of '. . . two or three gathered together . . .' in the name of the Lord may thus not only appear to occur but also be known to occur, because here we all are singing heartily, and mostly in tune and in time with the organist's necessarily just off-beat digitation. I am surely not alone in feeling deprived of a right to participate, even at King's College Chapel, Cambridge, when a choir sings for me and I and the rest of the congregation become mere members of an audience, the musical equivalent to 'church as museum'. A critical curiosity may then easily replace the wonder of worship. But participation by some members of a congregation does, however, not infrequently give rise to most unholy thoughts among others, which must justify the tradition for purists in King's College Chapel.

Great and appropriate but not necessarily solemn music, finely performed in suitable acoustics, can contribute notably to an elevation of spirit which occurs naturally to those amenable to the influence of the surroundings in most ancient, and in some modern, consecrated places. Acoustically, cathedrals and churches are not always ideal for music or even for speech. But just as the perpendicular and gothic styles of ecclesiastic architecture raise the eye above the horizon and may induce the mind to rise above the tedium, the suffering and the pettiness of our daily lives (if not also of the service itself), so music composed for performance in such resonant buildings sounds absolutely magnificent and helps to raise the spirits into the realm of Spirit.

For some people chanting seems to induce an hypnotic state as might any regular and prolonged rhythmic effect. I will not speculate as to whether a mystical experience results for such people or whether they are subject to mass hysteria of no religious significance. Is a mystical experience of religious significance? However that question might be answered, the use of music in chanting is frequently for an extra-musical purpose.

The Satyr's Family by Albrecht Dürer,
reproduced with the kind permission of
Gerd-Wolfgang Essen.
The mythological near-nuclear family in
an open-air domestic setting enjoy the
music of the pipe in the absence of a
wireless.

Mutus Liber in Quo Tamen.
Jacob asleep, called by angel-trumpeters
on the ladder—from the *Mutus Liber.*

The Flaying of Marsyas by Titian, Okresni Museum, Snemouni, Czechoslovakia—see pages 51-3, and footnote 4, page 56.

Venus and Mars by Botticelli, The National Gallery, London (c.1485).

Mischievous child satyrs play with the discarded armour and spear of a war-weary Mars. One of them blows a conch in Mars's ear. Mars may hear the sound as '...the dark music Blown from Sleep's trumpet' (see page 58) where he lies, naked and defenceless, a soft youth rather than a hardened warrior. A sweeter confrontation may await him, when he awakes. Serving Venus, the satyr children wield the spear as an erotic symbol of her cool will.

The Volga Boatmen by Ilya Repin, L'Hermitage, Leningrad—see page 108.

The Enraged Musician by Hogarth.
When I practise it is those within hearing who are more likely to be enraged.

The Thames at Twickenham by Peter Tillemans, Marble Hill House, Twickenham—see page 108.

David Harping before Saul by Rembrandt, Maurithuis Museum, The Hague (c.1658) — see pages 167-9.

HANDELSMAN FREAKY FABLES

Handelsman Freaky Fables, Punch, 15 May 1985.

Handelsman in his witty cartoon selectively summarizes the story of David and Saul—see pages 167-9 but in the first frame of the last line Handelsman, referring to Saul as having grown tired and slept in a cave, politely confuses the incident with another occasion when Saul's spear was removed while he slept, disregarding the Revised Version's description of Saul who went into the cave to 'cover his feet' (explained in *The Jerusalem Bible* as a euphemism(!) for 'to ease oneself'). David must have moved swiftly and very quietly to take advantage of Saul who was in reality caught short, not caught napping. (For another and fuller imaginative account of David's adventures see *God Knows* by Joseph Heller, Cape 1984.)

Self Portrait as a Deaf Man by Sir Joshua Reynolds, The Tate Gallery, London.
This extraordinarily poignant painting describes, without words, without self-pity, the
experience of all those who come to lose their hearing.

And then, to produce anything by art or craft 'to the glory of God' is in itself an activity of spiritual significance. Religion practised only in church is a contradiction in terms. Either God may be worshipped any- and everywhere – or nowhere. To sing 'And the glory, the glory of the Lord . . .' from Handel's *Messiah* is to participate in a common recognition of scale, of the magnitude of the Creator and of our insignificance save insofar as we can relate to Him, of man's inescapable reliance for his existence on forces over which he has not and will never have control. Whenever anyone forgets or denies that awe-inducing recognition he falls, and with him, to however small a degree, the whole of humanity. At the same time, what is made to the glory of God, effectively raises all humanity, be it a meal for the starving, a home for the destitute, a work of art or craft, or music. Belief in God or in gods, is not essential for this purpose, but a sense of scale and of man's relatively insignificant place in that scale is all-important.

It is hardly surprising that 'world religions' should claim a degree of universality. They appeal to the widest possible variety of people within the relevant 'catchment areas', be they largely national, cultural, racial or geographical. A world religion whose adherents were almost entirely from a particular economic or social class would be highly suspect. As a cultural opium for a middle-class constituency, an opium of convenience or for a peasant society, established religion is an opium supplied by those in power to keep the addicts subservient; it serves, for political power, as a stimulant to military or revolutionary action or counter-revolutionary repression. The Crusades, the Inqui- sition and the recent 'religious' takeover in Iran are historical examples of political action supposedly inspired by religious motives. This is not to be cynical about religion, but to recognize some realities of its socio-historical significance as distinct from its spiritual import.

To be effective for any purpose a religion, like any other body of ideas, sacred or secular, must attract adherents – and hold them. The forces which attract people may not be the same as those which retain their allegiance, as I have already indicated in respect of music-lovers who come to church. It is evident, however, that, in the case of any religion or religious sect, a variety of different features may be found initially attractive by different people and another variety may maintain their continuing communion. If all people were clones, with identical qualities, talents and aspirations there could be only one religion to fulfil the needs of all for anything that it might offer. As it is, the matter is vastly more complicated and interesting.

Each religion, each sect, presents a characteristic balance between the educational, ethical and spiritual elements in living on our planet, essential participants in the biosphere. As in the case of music, each element is likely to appeal differently: on the one hand to people whose psychological centre of gravity is worldly, functioning primarily through action, feeling or thought; and, on the other, to those whose centre of gravity is orientated more towards the development of spirituality.

Similarly music of various kinds will attract people who are open in different ways to its influences and to the power of religious ideas. A Salvation Army band apparently serves as a focal point to attract people who are amenable to the army's particular aims of worship through its form of discipline, its creed of self-denial and the demonstration of the meaning of compassion towards the needy. For the disciples of the Hari Krishna cult, jogging in diaphanous saffron garments up and down Oxford Street chanting and tapping their cymbals, music plays a different role, drawing attention to the rapt or 'lost' expressions on the faces of its adherents in case they would otherwise be ignored in the cosmopolitan, materialistically obsessed consumer crowd.

While music may serve the exoteric, manifest purposes I have described, any stimulation which may be derived from ordinary sense-perception is irrelevant to and a distraction from the path of spiritual enlightenment. For those who seek to follow such a path, the 'excitement', sometimes elation, and sheer pleasure of indulgence in playing and listening to music, as in the finest product of any art-form, as in the appreciation of the wonders of nature itself, must be transcended. Music can at best suggest or remind the attentive listener of non-material, relatively objective realities, stimulate, arouse and elevate rather than merely delight and excite; but it may thereby induce and provide a satisfaction which can stultify any care to go further, to look beyond it and to seek a destiny elsewhere. The joy, the comfort, the sense of mental and emotional gratification it may convey are not to be denigrated but music is not itself a spiritual exercise, for composer, performer or listener: it may guide those susceptible to its charms and powers towards a spiritual path but the path itself is still and silent, rich in another way.

[1] NAMKWA, Jonathan Cape, 1978.

[2] op. cit. p.150–1.

[3] C.G. Jung in his essay on 'The Tower', in *Memory, Dreams, Reflections* (Collins and Routledge & Kegan Paul 1963), refers to an experience which he ends up by describing as indescribable. It seems he was better equipped to portray visual rather than aural archetypes, to judge from this passage (Fontana edition, pages 255–6): 'I was in Bollingen . . . This was the winter of 1923–4. As far as I can recall, there was no snow on the ground; perhaps it was early spring. I had been alone perhaps for a week, perhaps longer. An indescribable stillness prevailed. One evening – I can still remember it precisely – I was sitting by the fireplace and had put a big kettle on the fire to make hot water for washing up. The water began to boil and the kettle to sing. It sounded like many voices, or stringed instruments, or even like a whole orchestra. It was just like polyphonic music, which in reality I cannot abide, though in this case it seemed to me peculiarly interesting. It was as though there were one orchestra inside the Tower and another one outside. Now one dominated, now the other, as though they were responding to each other. I sat and listened, fascinated. For far more than an hour I listened to the concert, to this natural melody. It was soft music, containing, as well, all the discords of nature. And that was right, for nature is not only harmonious; she is also dreadfully contradictory and chaotic. The music was that way too: an outpouring of sounds, having the quality of water and of wind – so strange that it is simply impossible to describe it.'

[4] Paul Griffiths, *The String Quartet*, Thames and Hudson, 1983.

[5] op.cit. p.158.

[6] '. . . Mother of the Free . . . God who made thee mighty, make thee mightier yet.'

9
FAMILIARITY

There is a mystery about different reactions to music, derived from the assortment of elements offered by music to meet variegated needs. We should not expect consistency in taste, yet may sometimes feel surprised when we discover that our own predilections and prejudices are not shared by others. Or we may be dismayed to find that our likes and dislikes coincide with the popular taste. Fortunately, a wide variety of choice is available to meet an almost unlimited range of preference, rejection and indifference – and willingness to listen to the previously unheard.

Familiarity does *not* breed contempt. It may engender appreciation or love, but only if that reaction is projected from one's own familiar qualities and they are themselves respected. Initial admiration for a work of art in any medium stems from a recognition of some distinction which resonated, as it were, with the mood of the moment, or appealed to a dominant taste. Familiarity discloses superficiality – unless it corresponds with a measure of one's own superficiality. On the other hand familiarity with a work which has some unusual features, without necessarily being 'deep' or 'profound', may enable one to perceive more than at first it seemed capable of conveying. In the case of a work which one found difficult or 'impossible' at first hearing – Beethoven's late quartets, Stravinsky's *Rite of Spring*, Bartok's six string quartets – persistence and attentive listening may open out new realms of musical and aesthetic experience.

As Shakespeare's Duke of Illyria says to introduce *Twelfth Night* (set by Purcell in alternative versions for a counter-tenor):

> If music be the food of love, play on;
> Give me excess of it, that, surfeiting,
> The appetite may sicken, and so die.
> That strain again! it had a dying fall:
> O, it came o'er my ear like the sweet sound,
> That breathes upon a bank of violets,
> Stealing and giving odour! Enough! no more:
> 'Tis not so sweet now as it was before.
>   . . .

But music is *not* the food of love, and the Duke was ruminating on the sweet agony of romantic love, not on music any more than on food. He was besotted with Olivia. It was a case of love at first sight. And so it can be with music, love at first hearing. But what we do not want then is 'excess of it, that, surfeiting, The appetite may sicken, and so die'. 'Nothing in excess' was the *other* inscription on the Temple of Apollo at Delphi. 'Know Thyself' alone was not enough.

When we find a piece of music exceptionally attractive, striking, even stunning, we will no doubt look forward to our next opportunity to hear it. If we shout 'encore' we do not always mean to invite an immediate repeat performance. We may want to hear the performer again or we may just be greedy. Familiarity with a particular musical work is not to be given a single simple definition. There are degrees of familiarity and they are bound to occur very differently for those who have learned to play an instrument, as distinct from those who can only listen.

We know how Orsino, the Duke of Illyria sought a cure for his love-sickness in too much music. Four days later (Act II Scene 4) he wants music again:

> Give me some music. Now, good morrow, friends
> No, good Cesario, but that piece of song,
> That old and antique song we heard last night:

Methought it did relieve my passion much,
More than light airs and recollected terms
Of these most brisk and giddy-paced times:
Come; but one verse.

Someone goes to fetch Feste, the jester, to sing it. Meanwhile, however, music is heard, while the Duke chats up Viola, shipwrecked and separated from her brother whom she fears may be drowned, and who is determined to help the Duke to win the love of Olivia, pining for her own dead brother. Viola is disguised as a boy, a eunuch in fact, for, as she says 'I can sing, And speak to him in many sorts of music. That will allow me very worth his service.' Their first conversation together proceeds –

Duke: Come hither, boy: if ever thou shalt love,
   In the sweet pangs of it remember me;
   For such as I am all true lovers are,
   Unstaid and skittish in all motions else,
   Save in the constant image of the creature
   That is beloved. How dost thou like this tune?
Viola: It gives a very echo to the seat
   Where love is throned.
Duke: Thou dost speak masterly:
   My life upon't, young though thou art, thine eye
   Hath stay'd upon some favour that it loves:
   Hath it not, boy?
Viola: A little, by your favour.

If the Duke were not completely deceived by Viola's disguise he might have guessed by her equivocal answers to his innocent probing that she is in love with him. Between these exchanges the Clown arrives and the Duke calls upon him to sing the song they'd had the night before, describing it to Viola as

. . . old and plain;
The spinsters and the knitters in the sun,
And the free maids that weave their thread with bones,
Do use to chant it: it is silly sooth,
And dallies with the innocence of love,
Like the old age.

Then the Clown sings a song difficult to recognize from that description, as if his aim were to mock and tease:

> Come away, come away, death,
>   And in sad cypress let me be laid;
> Fly away, fly away, breath;
>   I am slain by a fair cruel maid.
> My shroud of white, stuck all with yew,
>   O prepare it!
> My part of death, no one so true
>   Did share it.
>
> Not a flower, not a flower sweet,
>   On my black coffin let there be strown;
> Not a friend, not a friend greet
>   My poor corpse, where my bones shall be thrown:
> A thousand thousand sighs to save,
>   Lay me, O, where
> Sad true lover never find my grave,
>   To weep there!

'If dying be the food of love, slay on; Give me excess of it . . .'! Cheerful stuff. But *Twelfth Night* is not a comedy for nothing. Viola gets her Duke and he his 'mistress and his fancy's queen' in the end, leaving the Clown singing, like the Idiot at the end of *Boris Godunov* (Mussorgsky's ending, not Rimsky-Korsakov's) to philosophize, but about man's estate rather than the state of the nation.

Shakespeare was writing plays, not musicals (*Kiss Me Kate*, Cole Porter's delightful travesty of *The Taming of the Shrew*, notwithstanding). Hence he could introduce music for a song to convey a message outside the action of the play, a commentary in another dimension, on another scale. A profound message may be conveyed as effectively in a comedy as in an apparently more serious work or a tragedy. This is hardly surprising since the comic and the tragic are often separated by a fragile and invisible membrane. Indeed we may more easily miss the serious lesson in a tragedy, awed if not oppressed by solemn thoughts associated with self-pity than in a comedy where the ridiculous can free us for a while from our customary self-centredness; the serious is the more telling because of its contrast with

90

its comic background. 'Serious things cannot be understood without laughable things.'[1]

In music unadorned with words, however, any messages to be conveyed are more subtly communicated. If music is not just to lull our senses with a bland flavour, sweet, light or sour, it should surprise us, catch us out with the unexpected. At the same time what is unexpected will make a different kind of point if it is so incongruous as to distract our attention instead of alerting it.

Hence for a given piece of music, the frequency of repetition within a short period which one can bear will generally be proportionate to its complexity. There is more variety and more of the unexpected in Beethoven's *Waldstein* sonata than in a far shorter piece for piano, say a *Song Without Words* by Mendelssohn. It would be silly therefore to claim that one might not urgently need a change of aural environment given excess of any work, and surfeit would be likely to be reached sooner in the case of a shorter piece, say a Chopin waltz. If this musically vital element of the unexpected is lacking, the length of the piece is irrelevant to my point. But *over*-familiarity is, of course, excess.

With light or popular music – which must include much music by Telemann, Mozart and Vivaldi and by many others hardly less famous – even the relatively unexpected is rare. Such musical fare soon seems nauseating for anyone spoilt on a richer or more subtly flavoured diet. We may be astonished at the flow of familiar quotations in any of Shakespeare's better known plays but that will hardly dissuade us from sitting through them again and again. The famous quotes in isolation are telling, in themselves, but in their contexts make even better sense or, more often, illuminate ideas or relationships in complex but interesting ways. And that is exactly what unusual phrases, even notes, in music do, marking out every time genius from talent, perhaps the Beatles from Abba.

In a short work we *may* find a feast of emotional significance in a single cadence. But in the *Waldstein* our emotions are stretched over a canvas richly endowed with extremes which may leave us satisfied and probably re-energized. Memories and past emotional experiences will have been touched or stirred in an agreeable, exciting or disturbing way. The composer has played on our emotions, with enhanced and shattering logic. The process has been notably illuminated by that iconoclast and controversial teacher Hans Keller, especially in his analyses, by musical means alone, of chamber works by Mozart and

Beethoven. Those analyses, broadcast some years ago, have made clearer to me than any words, what correspondences and links sustain my interest through trails of complex musical strands which use the logic of sonata form flexibly. Hans Keller pointed up subtle reminders of inter-connections and the manner of their inter-play, constantly catching and holding my attention with an indication of the not so obvious cross-references which are there all the time.

It is not coincidence that had me quoting earlier from Shakespeare's *Pericles* and now from his *Twelfth Night*. In each, music is invoked, as from stars, heavenly spheres, to accompany a revelation of identity, a disclosure of a still extant relationship long assumed to have been severed by death.

There is a similar plot in *The Comedy of Errors* where music does not accompany the dramatic denouement. But in *The Tempest*, after Ariel sings 'Full fathom five thy father lies; . . .', music comes from where it should – 'This is no mortal business, nor no sound that the earth owes: – I hear it now above me' – from a place unknown to mortals.

Shackerley Marmion's epigram 'Familiarity begets boldness'[2] has a mite of truth in it, and more. When a kitten has made itself familiar with its immediate surroundings it extends the area of its exploration, glad of a base where it feels secure. So it is for listeners who are inspired to a measure of boldness from a base of familiar music such as the 'popular classics'.

If familiarity is the father, appetite is the mother of boldness. In itself there is no reason why familiarity should inspire an inclination to adventure. Some people who come to recognize as familiar not only the music they hear often but also any work in a similar style seem to need no more stimulating variety. For others, every opportunity to hear one thing leads fruitfully to another thing. The exploratory spirit is self-perpetuating.

But one person's 'turn-on' is another person's 'turn-off'. A single peep over the aural parapet and the timid may scuttle back to base till relieved by deafness or released by senility or death from the risk of re-exposure to the unfamiliar. Does the appetite change with an ever more varied diet on which it thrives, as does the taste of the music-lover who enjoys an ever-widening variety? We can appreciate the discovery of newly fascinating music while the staple diet of the relatively familiar works may continue to give pleasure, perhaps more pleasure, as a point of reference; or sampled only occasionally like pulp food and rusks when a child has a complement of teeth.

Some music is performed for the exhibition of a prodigious technique and not for musical content – music which may have been written solely as a vehicle for display. There is, nevertheless, music with more to it than appears from the technically brilliant performance without which it should not be heard in public at all. It would be too easy to dismiss as irrelevant the attraction of such works for those devoted to musical pyrotechnics but it would run counter to my aim to dismiss as meaningless any manifestation of musical expression which had significance for *any* listener.

Believing that *my* primary interest as a listener is not to discover the most brilliant or beautiful performance but its musical *content*, I recognize that this 'content' according to the score may seem significantly different in different performances – save that in a *recording* there cannot be any change at all in the interpretation.

Of course I expect performers faithfully to play the notes as written in the score, no more and no less. Yet I would allow a fair margin of interpretation in such matters as tempo and dynamics irrespective of the composer's own markings. These are not unimportant matters; on the contrary, they form the essential context in which the notes themselves may be variously performed and according to the taste, mood or whim of every performer in every performance, the very life-blood of music-making as distinct from note-spinning.

It is an element in a composition's greatness that it may be performed in a wide variety of different ways, each appealing *for purely musical reasons* to an audience. It is not necessary, indeed it is not to be expected that everyone who hears it will appreciate any particular performance – yet they may do. It may be thought that a critic wishing to show that he is doing his job must *almost* always find something to criticize; it would be easy, we may assume, for a critic to suggest how differently he would have preferred the performer to have played some phrase. But for the performer to have done so would have altered the context in which every other phrase was played and an interpreter of integrity must be allowed to know best. Any criticism of preference, involving an aesthetic, a value judgement is inevitably subjective: like any performance itself, it is at the same time both a partial view and a whole view – for performer and critic. It will tell us something about the critic and little about the performer and nothing certain about the composer. That this apparent paradox holds true for every member of an audience – every listener his own critic, and his own vicarious performer, as it were – renders the whole greater than the sum of the parts. Until the last performance of any work there can be no objective whole assessment; yet all the partial views are, independently, objective wholes for each occasion to which they refer.

The 'amateur listener' may take for granted a critic's far greater musical experience, but should not burden even – or especially – a reputable critic with the expectation that he is capable of an objective judgement. Yet I would promote the theoretical ideal of a final assessment by an omniscient being able to take account of every less than objective assessment of any musical work and any performance along the way.

It seems to me axiomatic that 'Western' music communicates with each of us as emotional beings. At the same time I recognize that certain elements in some music appeal intellectually, logically. We may not go all the way with Anthony Hopkins when he discusses the first movement of Mozart's piano sonata in C (K.309) but we will surely find some validity in his style of analysis and conclusions.[3]

Hopkins draws attention to Mozart's 'ingenuity in handling basically conventional ideas' by exploiting contrasts of texture and volume and leading us 'into supposing we can anticipate what is going to happen next – whereupon Mozart does something different . . .' Anthony Hopkins finds one phrase 'positive and masculine; it is instantly followed by a yielding, feminine response that serves to remind us of the essentially operatic nature of so much of Mozart's thought'. If that is stating the obvious, the same is true of so much of all composers' thoughts! But is it? Not by any means can all music which is not avowedly programmatic be designated programmatic by association.

Pursuing this operatic analogy he provides an imaginary libretto, for his supposed male and female characters, in contrasting phrases (finding the female much more long-winded) until the female 'appears to rush upstairs' to escape her cruel rejection by the man. As the work is a piano sonata and not an opera it is the imaginative – not imaginary – evocation of the emotional meaning of the phrases which each listener experiences. We may speculate as to whether the impact is more effective in the absence of words than if Mozart had composed the same music as a song, a concert aria or part of an opera. But that will enlighten us not at all. If the chosen form is effective for its intended purpose, in any other form its purpose would be at least subtly different. Many of the greatest classical composers – at random (almost) Haydn, Bach, Handel, Mozart, Beethoven and Schubert – employed similar themes and similar tunes in a number of different forms or settings. Turner frequently included the sun in his paintings, and Constable a certain farmer's dog; Rembrandt painted many self-portraits and Monet caught numerous impressions of light on his waterlilies, the towers of Rouen Cathedral and Charing Cross Bridge, and Cézanne painted Mont Sainte-Victoire over and over again. No one complains of having seen them before.

A fresh impression of the matter can be gained, for each of us, by an approach from the inside, that is from the experiences of our own emotional lives. For our emotions our music, and the paintings, provide a correspondence – reflection and resonance. It seems that our lives consist mostly of swift reactions to stimuli of various kinds. We are at most barely conscious of the stimuli, many of them subliminal – sounds, gestures, inflexions, smells – some from involuntary inner bodily activities and others from the subconscious, day-dreams, or 'intuition'. We are equally unaware of our reactions to most of these multitudinous flashes of stimulation. Indeed, it is as if our so-called conscious mind is largely shielded by protective devices of the nervous system; otherwise we would be overwhelmed.

James Joyce in his monumental *Finnegans Wake* was doing much more than simulate at length a stream of consciousness. That alone would not encompass a complete-in-itself work of art, a tone poem in words of super-symphonic dimensions and contrapuntal form. Words made up of letters are not emotions any more than are musical phrases made up of notes – whether the words are only written or actually spoken or sounded. But either notes or words can touch on, can possibly evoke, emotions as they pass the portals of perception.

And that is a major, perhaps *the* major apparent function of music – to stimulate emotions or, more often, memories of emotions. Words, especially in poetry, *may* serve a similar purpose but often the associations they invoke only stimulate word-sequences; the emotional element itself seems to provoke fresh and more elaborate or forceful verbalization. And that is less relaxing and releasing than the stimulation of non-verbal memories of emotions and, less frequently, an immediate emotional experience.

It is as if our hidden, stored emotional life lies like a large family of sea anemones on a seabed, with tentacles waving gently in the water, waiting to latch on to a passing consumable morsel and to thrust it towards the digestive system; or at any intimation of hostility to draw in all tentacles instantly and close the outer skin. Our emotional anemones respond with expectant sensitivity to a fluid expanse of music. The tentacles of each creature are alert to the promise of stimulation. But the creatures are each sensitive to slightly different emotional stimuli; or in terms of this analogy what is an attractive digestible morsel to one creature may be of no interest or may even be repellent to another. Hence, in musical terms, one man's meat . . . – and within each listener some nexus of emotion will welcome what others find anathema. But the responses activated by the movement of music will vary according to the mood and conditioning of the person from or within whom they emanate.

The appropriate music will hypnotize or animate some of these emotional sea anemones and evoke a response which contributes to a feeling of well-being in the subject. This feeling may resonate for a while after the actual sound of the music has ceased. Another work heard during this period of emotional resonance may reinforce the effect, or may cut across and break it up, leaving the subject restless or irritated, unsatisfied or dissatisfied.

We take it for granted that a sonata, symphony, concerto or any other extended work comprising several movements has been composed as a unity each movement of which 'belongs' in the whole. Anyone conditioned by familiarity with all of Beethoven's symphonies would probably feel uncomfortable if a performance were given of first, second, third and fourth movements each from a different symphony. That would be a doomed test, because such a person would know at the start of the second movement that something was wrong. It would be hard to find anyone musically sophisticated enough to assess the rightness or otherwise of an incorrect juxtaposition of movements who has not heard the raided symphonies already, each performed rightly as a whole.

As Beethoven developed the symphonic form through the corpus of his symphonies so his style matured, enabling him to extend symphonic form and language and to encompass ideas of greater complexity and emotional depth and range. But more significant is the distinct prevailing mood of each symphony, the even-numbered symphonies being relatively relaxed and 'sunny' and the odd-numbered symphonies (after the first) being directed to more heroic, turbulent or 'serious' themes. Musical characteristics are unmistakable in any work by a composer gifted enough to have developed his own style – and there is little of lasting merit to be found in any composer's pastiche music. It would be helpful to an understanding of my point if every composer of integrity could be relied upon, unlike Bach in his suites for example, to compose every movement of any work to relate specifically to the music of all the other movements in the same work. However themes and phrases may occasionally appear recognizably or may, in various disguises, have been woven deliberately or instinctively into the fabric of a piece. Hence the suspicion that a Frankenstein monster of a symphony put together from disparate movements taken from different symphonies, even by the same composer, could not 'work', that each transplanted 'limb' would reject the others. Nevertheless where key relationships were 'correct' or the interspersed movements suitably transposed, a Frankenstein surgeon would often get away with it. We are conditioned by hearing works played, in respect of their movements, as the composers intended: memory patterns have been laid down which trigger a wish to reject a change. We are not truly free to choose what we think sounds best since it can never sound right.

As the test of a 'great work' on the listener is subjective, an inner sympathy with the composer will have special importance. Although this will apply in general, perhaps only for a certain period in the life of a given listener, on any particular occasion a chance association or the listener's mood may dictate an unaccustomed preference for the music of a composer usually shunned, and *vice versa*. What might be termed temperamental differences – for example my two friends' opposite reaction to the music of Brahms when they were depressed – can be understood as resulting from the different effects of depression, or of Brahms on their respective groups of emotional sea anemones.

It must be clear that a tremendous responsibility falls on anyone who arranges the programme for a concert, the items to be included and the order in which they will be performed. Of course, a programme may be constructed to demonstrate an historical succession or the plums of a visiting conductor's repertoire. But a truly satisfactory programme will be designed to take into consideration an audience's relative unity of taste, and within that rough calculation will generate and seek to accumulate and conserve a degree of emotional unity.

This effect may be achieved as well by the relaxation of tension of a meaningful anticlimax as by a climactic conclusion. After the tumultuous variety of Mahler's *Song of the Earth* the ending is compelling, as it fades away to the word 'Ewig' (Ever) repeated ever softer, in the power of its message. Sibelius finishes his fifth symphony no less effectively in an entirely different way, with two striking chords played fortissimo; but William Walton, a great admirer of Sibelius, ends his first symphony with a coda which appears to occupy half the last movement – a sergeant-major's order 'Wait for it!' never prolonged frustration so cruelly. For me it long outstays its welcome while the composer seems to be trying against the odds to bring the movement and the symphony to an end. Still that is better than the unsatisfactory anticlimax of a conventional, too easily anticipated ending. And Tchaikovsky's *1812* overture is worse than the Walton.

The point and the question is, what, as a result of any musical experience, happens to the emotional life of the audience. Curiously the sense of satisfaction which justifies any musical activity does not require everyone to leave a concert in a state of elation. Music is more likely to offer, in respect of emotions which tend to the manic or the depressed, *sublimation* – a recollection of the emotion itself rather than a re-experiencing of it. It is as if we are more likely to be stirred by music to recall extremes of emotion or imagine them. We get a taste of those emotions at a lower, bearable level of intensity than is provided by the actual experiences of them.

When discussing variations of interpretation earlier in this chapter I was writing with a solo pianist or violinist in mind. In expanding the theme of the impact of music on the emotions I transferred my focus to symphonies, I referred to concerts and intended to leave no impression that the effects I was describing would be as evident when listening to a recording or even a live broadcast. Who can have failed to notice how a concert consisting of a well-chosen programme, admirably performed in a hall with excellent acoustics seems to fall flat if the hall is half empty? The generation, accumulation and conservation of emotional experiences simply does not occur. We are saddened and feel sorry for the performers. Applause peters out embarrassingly however energetically we may clap. There are insufficient enthusiasts to maintain the same level of applause when any start to flag.

Something similar may happen to our emotional anemones if too few of them are activated, that is if too narrow an emotional range is stirred to promote a tension of expectancy across a wide emotional expanse. This would explain why in a mood of sadness or happiness most listeners would not seek 'sad' or 'happy' music. A vicarious reminder through music of a wider range of emotions than is actually being experienced seems somehow more satisfying than a closer correspondence. It seems that a reverie *about* sadness or happiness is stimulated by music. Then the question whether or not the music helps one out of a sad mood, if that were for certain desirable, or destroys a mood of happiness, if that were a matter for regret, is irrelevant; the mood may remain because it is experienced directly as compared with the weaker distorted quality of recollection. Some people seem generally happy and others generally pensive or solemn or sad, but it does not follow that any valid deduction can be made as to the mood of the music which each would be likely to favour. The needs or appetites of a person's inner emotional life for the 'reminder' are mysterious. My own needs and appetites seldom bear any clear relationship to the outward expressions of my emotions. Only an exceptionally percipient and sympathetic outside observer could recognize the discrepancies, of which, as a rule, I am barely aware myself.

As we should expect, however, there are correspondences between one's inner life and the outward expression of it. Have not we all known our own moods of restlessness and a thirst or hunger for an unspecified change? Then, when it comes, we may not like it, we long for the return of easier, less exciting or at least less eventful days. When indeed are the times *not* 'out of joint' for one or another part of our complex beings? To be in turn anxious, flattered, disappointed, fearful, bored, hopeful, angry, regretful, pressed – an almost endless list – is, from the point of view of our emotions, a description of our lives. One does not have to be a manic-depressive to know something of the swings between these two extremes on no matter how modest a scale they operate. Sometimes a blacker or a lighter mood may last for days, at others for only seconds, but not a moment passes without some emotional content. A strong emotion will take over and rule until it blows itself out of energy or is effectively distracted, but weak ones mutter and grumble most of the time, noticed only by other people until they communicate a complaint.

It is into this environment, weird because we are generally unaware of it and at the same time natural to virtually all people in a complex and confused culture such as ours, that music is invited and has its effect. If it were unwanted by all, it would not be tolerated let alone welcomed. Of course some choose to inflict it on others who would prefer silence or only the natural sounds of the environment, or who do not want the particular music imposed on them. But if we confine our investigation to the concern of those who seem to want music we may usefully enquire *why* they do.

In referring to 'those who seem to want' music I implied that there are those who positively want it and those who do not. But these simple alternatives ignore the reality of our largely unnoticed emotional lives, lives whose frequent and rapidly changing moods dictate our expressed desires. 'I feel like a drink!' 'Good idea!' That not unusual exchange in our society might be understood by a visitor from outer space, familiar with our language only literally, to mean 'Coincidentally these two humans experience a thirst for liquid refreshment.' It (the alien creature) would be both right and wrong. The message exchanged, from *inner* space, between the human beings meant, as *they* understood, that they wanted to engage in relaxed social intercourse assisted, as convention dictates in their social milieu, by an alcoholic beverage. So they only *seemed* to want 'a drink'.

Similarly, we might usefully distinguish between wanting to listen to music and only seeming to want to do so – maybe wanting to hear it but not wanting to listen to it. Often one has no choice in the matter because there is music in the air where one happens or has chosen to be for other reasons than to listen to it. Music may be a background to a meal in a restaurant; this in itself is different from choosing to have music as a background in one's own home.

If I must eat out alone, will I choose to go where there is background music and if so will it make a difference what *sort* of music it is – never mind what specific music? The answer to such legitimate questions will very likely depend on where it is or who is with me, or on 'my mood'. Of course if I am alone I can have something handy to read, or even a notepad, but otherwise may I not be especially aware of my aloneness, with others in company on separate tables around me? A meal is traditionally a social occasion as well as a physical necessity; for habitually gregarious people, to eat alone in public is to flaunt their loneliness. One is engaged in observing the surroundings with particular care but no particular attention, and in observing other people within the ambit of polite behaviour, that is noticing, by looking without appearing to do so. There is a ceaseless inner conversation and emotions fluctuate in intensity and switch between a guilty, half-suppressed self-pity and feelings for and against the others present according to one's impressions of them filtered through acquired attitudes.

In such a grim ambience music can serve several purposes. It enables one to avoid the discomfort of one's inner babble in the midst of but detached from the outer babble. The isolation which might be painful is sensed as only relative after all. The music provides a binding force for the whole company, irrespective of the significance to any individual present of what is actually played.

On the same occasion in the restaurant those who are eating specifically with someone else share effects of the music with the loners, but enjoy or endure other effects too. Music may be too loud for comfortable conversation. But that can be a relief where over-exposure, as in the course of a marriage between conversational incompatibles – or ultra-compatibles – renders virtual silence inevitable but still embarrassing in public, or when verbal intercourse may have to be avoided because it could not disguise the manifestation of exceptionally powerful and disagreeable emotions – ennui, bickering, grief or fury, perhaps. The same music may cover the exchanges of true – and half-true and untrue – lovers which are more tellingly conveyed by the clasping of hands and by the engaging of eyes. And for those who want to gossip or to discuss something seriously music can provide an invisible aural screen to allow adults to be seen and not overheard.

I share the traditional reservations of purists about the ethics of inflicting the pernicious pollution of background music on anyone, anywhere, at any time. Yet I recognize the point of this pervasive noise and the right of any restaurateur to determine whether the acoustics of his premises and the anticipated or assumed preferences of his clientele justify its use. In shops, hotels, pubs and public transport its introduction is pressed by commercial interests. If it is fulfilling a public need, though not necessarily a need of every member of the public, this is a measure of the need in our society for tranquillizers. In public places people may have been found easier to manage and manipulate for the greater convenience of management and the greater profit of commercial entrepreneurs.

Music-as-background must always be or seem to be familiar. Music-to-attend-to acts differently on us according to its content, to our familiarity with it and to the attention we give to it. We might have heard several hundred of Vivaldi's 450 or so concertos and each several times; we should then be forgiven for regarding yet another one, which we had not previously heard 'familiar'. Though in reality it was new to us, we would certainly be familiar with the style and idiom. The point is, that if we felt at home with Vivaldi's concertos as background music we would not feel less at home or more, with any one of his concertos heard for the first or the umpteenth time.

We may imagine that composers after Vivaldi, Haydn, Bach and Mozart were less prolific and may not be so easy to take for granted because subsequent music developed more rapidly in complexity and in the exploration of fresh idioms. Such a proposition is dubious. Beethoven notably extended the range of musical expression, but so did Haydn; Wagner can hardly be said to have developed in musical maturity further or faster than Mozart. We may know 'quite well' only half a dozen of Mozart's forty-one symphonies and a few dozen of Schubert's 600 or so, far shorter, songs but we have heard at most, probably three or four of the thirty-two symphonies of Havergal Brian, a neglected British composer who died in 1972 a few years short of his century. Brian has been little performed partly because of his extravagance with orchestral forces, expensive to muster and needing far more than customary rehearsal time, and partly because his rich orchestration has been for some time unfashionable in the absence of such useful signposts as easily recognizable tunes.

If I had heard enough to qualify me to discuss its implications this survey might be extended into the realm of electronic music and the use of electronics to extend the sounds and vocabulary of 'ordinary' instrumentation. But I doubt whether it would provide examples significantly different in kind from those of contemporary composers who use conventional instruments in new combinations and in new ways, since economic factors apply with equal significance. Some composers have required special preparation of a piano for a particular work, e.g. Henry Cowell and John Cage, and virtuoso instrumentalists in close collaboration with a few modern composers have discovered new ways of playing stringed and woodwind instruments in particular, e.g. George Crumb, Berio and Stockhausen who have written works for the oboist Heinz Holliger; music has been composed to incorporate the new sounds musically, not merely to demonstrate the discoveries.

It is hard for anyone with even a half-musical ear to fail to have his attention attracted, however adverse the circumstances, by a work in an idiom with which he is unfamiliar, if it is of any musical significance. I remember listening spellbound to a performance of Bartok's violin concerto, now known as his second, broadcast during the war, the dedicatee, Menuhin, being the soloist. At the time, the summer of 1943, I was an army liaison officer attached to the RAF on a Night Fighter Station in the Midlands. I was in the officer' mess playing a game of chess. I do not recall what happened to the game (I never was more than a wood-shifter anyway) but my attention was captivated by the power, the coherence and beauty of the work, and at the same time I was in trepidation lest someone with us in the mess would get up, exlaim 'God, what an awful row' and switch it off.

Those were not the best conditions for first or ever listening to such a work – pretending to give attention to a game and all the time fearing that the exhilarating experience of the music would be rudely terminated at any moment. But the tensions were mostly external to my empathy with the music itself. Each person will experience differently from others the impact of new music, music immediately distinguishable from anything he has heard before though not necessarily in a completely strange idiom. On second hearing an increase rather than decrease of tension may, however, be experienced by anyone listening with attention. On the first occasion everything is unexpected. On each subsequent hearing more and more features will be recognized and their position in relation to the journey from beginning to end roughly noted, until the listener's mind has a fairly complete map of the whole route. For me there is a special tension I associate with the gradual filling in of such a map. Some works have left me seemingly little wiser at the end of many hearings, yet still willing to persevere with an inexplicable faith that the effort is worthwhile, e.g. Elliott Carter's first string quartet or Brian Ferney-hough's sonatas for string quartet. I find other works become progressively less interesting with repeated hearings, for example the music of Messiaen.

Of course this feeling of tension enhances one's pleasure in concert performances. Even in the case of very familiar works, interpretation by a great conductor or performer is *always* desirable, but seldom achieved. It produces anew that sense of uncertainty which is so pleasurable when one can be reasonably confident that, however unexpected a phrase or a whole movement may be, played in the hands of this master it will seem somehow right, or throw new and interesting light on the music itself. There really is no need to become involved in speculation about the composer's intentions – let alone any question of his 'real intentions'; or to read programme notes or listen to BBC comparative analyses.

With any luck, to be attracted to a concert to hear for the second or third time a work found interesting, even exciting, on first hearing, enables one to hear some other composition for the first time. Unimaginative concert programme-building may increasingly impede this desirable progression which otherwise proclaims the truth of that epigram 'Familiarity begets boldness.'

In the British Isles, not to be a Londoner is no excuse since for over thirty years Radio 3 and its predecessor the Third Programme have supplied live and recorded performances of a range far wider than can be mounted in any series or season of public concerts. There is little to lose by yielding to temptation to explore on record music heard first on the radio or music by a composer whose other work has ever given you a moment of pleasurable surprise. If the crystallized performance on record eventually palls, when the mind's ear anticipates everything exactly, then you may find yourself keen to have recordings of other performances for comparison, till space to store and time to listen cruelly limit any extension of the process.

Meanwhile there will be ample scope to experiment with your own programme-planning. By perusal of the daily forecasts of radio programmes, chosen records from your collection can be interpolated into an evening of random offerings by the blessed BBC.

With a wide enough choice available, anyone can begin to see what impels his own selection on any occasion. I have previously referred to the concert promoter or arranger of programmes of broadcast music who apportions significance to, and balances such relevant factors as available resources both musical and financial, the implications of possible clashes with or duplications of the same works performed or broadcast contemporaneously, the taste and repertoire of the proposed conductor and any soloist, the relative dictatorship of the box-office or listener ratings, and so on. In the same way the home programme-planner will want to time selected recorded works to fit into the gaps between any selected broadcast works and, in a good mood, perhaps the convenience of a meal with other members of the household, in the preparation or disposal of which he – or she – should, in common courtesy, assist. To include the most recently acquired recordings or those not played for some while, whose special qualities may therefore have been forgotten or only half remembered, may tempt collectors who share my curious characteristic of feeling a kind of pity for neglected things as well as for rejected people.

While I have already emphasized the significance of the 'reminder' element in one's emotional response to music there is another 'reminder' factor of increasing influence on one's selection of music-to-listen-to-next. Some people are fairly described as butterflies for settling wherever they do for *just long enough* for their natural purposes, unless disturbed. There is surely no evidence that it is distractions which persuade the insects to move on. With but a little effort at self-observation, without self-criticism or self-justification, any of us can observe how quickly, in contrast, *our* minds are distracted. Sense impressions and ideas 'coming from nowhere' have our attention darting and jumping with remarkable rapidity between our perceptions and apparently random thoughts and day-dreams. The human butterfly is skilled at avoiding the evidence of this state of mind.

Deryck Cooke in *The Language of Music* gave examples to show how the same or similar musical phrases are used, beyond the nature of coincidences, by different composers, in quite different kinds of works, to convey the same meanings. It is arguable that this occurs through association with what has been heard previously, so that use of a particular phrase is inevitable in a particular context because the composer's conditioned mind naturally produces the musical equivalents of an egg to fit an egg-cup. In each instance there is room for a small range of variation. In each case a specific but undefined *feeling* is conveniently established.

Whatever the true causation, I believe Deryck Cooke regarded the connections between the musical phrases and the emotional meaning to be archetypal rather than conditioned, and he might be right. It is odd, beyond the possibility of coincidence and outside the range of likely conditioning, that Fauré introduces the same cadence in the 'Libera Me' section of his *Requiem* as is sung in the Negro spiritual *Let My People Go.*

The process of familiarization is the passive conditioning which enables the listener to identify music he has heard before. The recognition of similarities of style, the evidence of historical development and ever more of the cross-references which abound in music, are among its special felicities. Mozart and Rossini may quote Mozart in operas just as Alban Berg quotes Bach in his violin concerto and Charles Ives quotes in many of his works popular songs and hymns and tunes for brass bands and, in his monumental second piano sonata, *Concord Mass., 1840–60*, a phrase from Beethoven's fifth symphony. Beethoven based his adagio variations and rondo, Op.121A, for violin, cello and piano *Ich bin der Schneider Kakadu* on a popular song from Wenzel Muller's musical, *Die Schwestern von Prag*, Bach adopted a tune composed by Martin Luther, Brahms wrote sets of variations on themes of Handel, Haydn, Schumann and Paganini and Mendelssohn quotes hymns with Roman Catholic and Lutheran associations in the first and last movements respectively of his fifth, *Reformation*, symphony. Fifty of Beethoven's contemporaries were invited to contribute one variation each on a waltz composed by Diabelli to promote his music-publishing business – but we know of this only from history books and Beethoven's set of 33 variations Op.120 which have alone rendered Diabelli's uninspired little tune memorable beyond its wildest deserts. The list could be long enough to impress even the most pure Purist capable of demanding *complete* originality from any composer with a claim to be considered great.

Of course the process of importation extends far beyond the borrowings of composers from their own music and others'. Jazz idiom and instrumentation has entered into the 'classical' repertoire through, for example, music by Bartok (concerto for orchestra), Stravinsky, Copland, Bernstein, Martinu, Constant Lambert, Walton, Milhaud, Vaughan Williams. Famous musicians have experimented with a merging of the musical-cultural streams. Johnny Dankworth improvised under Raymond Leppard's direction with Yehudi Menuhin and together they played William Russo's music for violin and jazz orchestra. In his autobiography, *Unfinished Journey*,[4] Menuhin describes his fruitful collaboration with Stephane Grappelli. He regarded 'the great jazz violinist' as his mentor 'on a journey to spontaneity'. This path, Menuhin says, was for him 'always latent; as probably it is for other violinists'. I wonder about that.

Menuhin wrote that in recording sessions, Grappelli never repeated himself: 'Off the cuff [he] can use any theme to express any nuance – wistfulness, brilliance, aggression, scorn – with a speed and accuracy that stretch credulity.' If that is what Grappelli can do improvising what need is there for composed music? An interesting question to consider with its implications, with Menuhin's aspiration to begin a journey towards spontaneity.

Meanwhile there are several obvious examples of cross-fertilization. Ravi Shankar, as Menuhin relates, has participated in concerts aiming to bridge the idioms of Western and Indian music. Such efforts require adaptability and an openness to listening beyond that required of all musicians who play in ensembles. It is hardly surprising then that such efforts are rare, in public at least.

In composed music there are very many examples of importation of idioms from other cultures and styles. Some, in the event, sound acceptable and others either pretentious or bogus. As with attempts to reproduce 'authentic' ancient music, great music-making may result from – or in spite of – a high degree of compromise. So we may find any Chinese element in Mahler's *Song of the Earth* little more than incidental when the music itself is at the same time thrilling and profound. Ravel's *Chansons madecasses* I find powerfully evocative of the (imagined) exotic East – perhaps because I have never visited Madagascar or because the accompaniment of cello, flute and piano is so effective. The equally exotic element in *Flos Campi* by Vaughan Williams matches that of *Schelomo* by Bloch. A Near-Eastern ancestry may give no special advantage in conveying the ambience of that area; inspiration may overcome any such influence, be it an advantage or a disadvantage.

More often than not the setting may seem to be quite irrelevant to the music for an opera, a song-cycle, tone-poem or any work which is located somewhere remote from the composer's indigenous or adopted surroundings. It really doesn't matter that we are no more impressed with a supposedly Italianate idiom or sentiment in Berlioz' symphonic study, *Harold in Italy* than in Mendelssohn's *Italian* symphony – or Respighi's *Fountains of Rome*. They are simply pieces in the European Romantic tradition. Dvorak in his *New World Symphony* introduced, in symphonic form, musical themes which emanated from North America, as he did also in his American string quartet, tactfully so re-named a few years ago. 'Foreign' themes are often fruitfully introduced into a piece imprinted with the composer's own idiom and the overriding style of his time and culture.

True folk-music – music derived from a purely aural tradition, inevitably with definable local characteristics – may portray surprising geographical links and has had an extraordinary influence on sophisticated Western music. From Bach to Haydn, Beethoven to Bartok, the transformation of folk-music is certain if not always obvious. In Russian and Czech and twentieth-century English music the direct influence of folk-music *is* obvious and therefore, perhaps, becomes precious and tiresomely repetitious. Every Russian composition (I theorize with only slight exaggeration) – represents the Great Gate of Kiev or is a variation on the Volga boatman's song. The boatmen were sad tramps and simpletons, dragging boats along the towpath of the Volga. Surprisingly, I have been unable to trace a similar work-song used by the Thames boatmen on their towpath.[5]

In the early years of this century some English composers seemed to be dominated by a folk idiom: Ireland, Butterworth, Moeran, Bax and Grainger among others. Vaughan Williams is interesting by comparison. Up to the sixth symphony his musical personality usually transcended the folk-music element, one of the joys of his music being his distillation of fruitful influences from early church music imbued or combined with the folk element, as in his *Fantasia on a Theme of Tallis* and his fifth symphony. Holst's flirtation with Eastern ideas may have helped *him* to a healthy independence. Such independence was attained also, through other influences and instincts, by Gerald Finzi, Bridge and subsequently Britten.

Now it is suggested by some musicologists that the impact of folk-music is waning among contemporary composers, preoccupied with the exploration of new realms of sound. That may be so for some composers. Listeners generally show more conservative tastes, preferring, it seems, the best familiar music, relying on 'good' tunes, that can be recognized when heard again and contain the germ of something hummable and 'agreeable' harmonies. Such harmonies may these days include chords which were formerly regarded as discords and so were, almost by definition, disagreeable. I believe that, for audiences, the absorbed, transformed and transcended folk-music will continue to satisfy an underlying need to feel a connection with cultural roots.

How could it be otherwise if I were right to regard folk-tunes as in the nature of archetypal symbols in musical terms. With contemporary 'serious' composers I have had a long-lasting sympathetic relationship as a supporter for many years of the Society for the Promotion of New Music. I do not attempt to predict how music the SPNM promotes will be regarded in the future – if it has a future. There is not yet enough of it composed *and* performed to justify such speculation. But much of the composition of young or relatively unknown composers whose music the society seeks to promote remains firmly entrenched in the classical tradition which can never completely deny its folk origins and indebtedness to aural transmission from antiquity.

So classical, 'serious' music will continue to attract performances and audiences for whom the folk idiom may be archetypal and anyway retains a flavour of familiarity for all who listen to it. The far larger audience hearing such music chiefly in debased, i.e. over-simplified, repetitive forms as the popular music of the day, light, dance and film music, is, if anything, more securely trapped. Whatever we may understand of certain music as archetypal, it is founded essentially on tunes which reflect deep-seated emotions and moods – including the mood to dance with gaiety and abandon, or with daemonic intensity as epitomized in Stravinsky's *Les Noces* and *Rite of Spring* – two works written for ballet which especially attract me as pure music, powerful and original. There's a musical snob for you! But the point is that they grow in interest with repeated hearings. When I listen to *these* works without the visual element I do not personally miss the dancing as if it were an essential ingredient in a complete integrated art-form.

Hence I perceive as a virtue of familiarity with a specific musical work, the power to remind me of its refreshing elements. These elements enable me to bear without complaint whatever degree of repetition is inflicted on me, or I choose to inflict on myself, after the first interest of relative unfamiliarity has expired. A listener's surprise at the ending of a masterpiece lasting less than ten minutes, say Anton Webern's symphony Op.21, so soon after the beginning,

109

just as the listener is feeling some sense of familiarity with its idiom, may be a measure of *his* genius.

---

[1] Gurdjieff, at his Institute for Harmonious Development of Man, Fontainbleau.

[2] From his play *The Antiquary* (*Oxford Dictionary of Quotations*).

[3] *Understanding Music*, J. M. Dent, 1979; a chapter entitled 'Purpose and Method'.

[4] Macdonald and Jane's, 1977.

[5] See illustration section.

10
SPONTANEITY

The title of Menuhin's autobiography, *Unfinished Journey*, is obviously appropriate for a not yet completed lifetime of music-making. It also reflects ceaseless efforts generously to repay, by teaching, by example and above all with humanity, the debt of gratitude he acknowledges for his exceptional talents, and the good fortune of a happy and a fulfilling life. It requires no special intuitive powers to infer from his choice of title that he is referring to another journey than that traversed in the course of a lifetime.

Menuhin describes Ravi Shankar and Stephane Grappelli as 'successive mentors on a journey to spontaneity'. A few sentences earlier he had written: 'The phrase "It's the gypsy in me", generally offered in extenuation of disorderly conduct, bears witness . . . to a need wider than mine alone for the refreshment of living with the moment as if one had never known it before. Perhaps because I was by temperament or training inclined, even at the crest of a wave, to calculate its amplitude and momentum, I have always thirsted for abandon. Just as yoga promised release from physical impediments, so improvisation promised abandon to musical impulse.' And a little later: 'To reach our apogee, we have to subjugate our natures, then to free them. In the venture, each tradition, the extempore and interpretative, can help the other, and those musicians who synthesize the two are the most complete, the worthiest of our admiration . . . As I have suggested, the lines of my life are mostly simple, rounding the circle where they are not straight.' There he leaves the subject of the other journey.

But I cannot. It is germane precisely to my quest, through an examination of what music means to me, in relation to my aim to know myself. If Menuhin's journey takes him through the experience of joint-improvisation towards spontaneity may not a music-loving listener seek spontaneity through listening-in-a-new-way?

Starting at the age of fifty-three to learn to play the violin, when the co-ordination of muscle and ear are not as acute or immediate as for a much younger beginner, I realize how essential is the sheer concentration on the bare rudiments of technique. Without technique there seems no scope to express or develop musicality. I try so hard to read and to play the notes better than approximately, to place and move the bow 'correctly', to relax, to remember to do this and that all at once and in sequence, that the sounds I encourage or enable the fiddle to make I hardly hear.

While my efforts are devoted to getting things 'right' my feeling for the music, be it a study, a Rodé caprice, or a movement of a Bach partita, is nowhere. Yet the pleasure attained through my struggle with the Bach as, thirty years earlier, I had struggled with the first three of Bach's cello suites, is intense. I can arrive home in the evening weary from my professional day. I tackle Bach – no, I *embrace* him, and at the same time shamefully ignore him – and fatigue, anxiety and depression are magicked away. However much pleasure I derive from practising other music it does not bestow on me the blessing of elation as does Bach. Karl Barth is reported to have said 'When the angels play for God they play Bach; but when they play for themselves they play Mozart . . . and God eavesdrops.' Whatever the experience of others, that is a wittily perceptive epigram.[1]

Yet who would call Bach's music 'spontaneous'? It seems as deliberately composed as the work of anyone. It is intellectually satisfying and, to one who approaches music intellectually as I have done to a marked degree, it is at the same time emotionally 'elevating'.

With Bach-induced elation some different element enters into my experience – something different in kind and not merely in quality from the numerous and varied pleasures to be derived from the music of other composers. Some of Bartok's great works such as *Bluebeard's Castle*, string quartets two to five, the second sonata for violin and

112

piano and his piano suite Op.14, provide an experience close to that induced by Bach's music; but in writing *that* I am reverting to my role as listener. Listening to Bach is nowhere near as emotionally effective as playing his works, and I have not attempted to play Bartok hence the artificiality of the comparison. That Bartok's music does not consistently or reliably touch me as powerfully as Bach's may be attributable to the gloomy edge of much of Bartok's output. There seems to be in the music of both of them an exceptional integrity. Unlike in the music of Bach, Bartok's pessimism, though not distraught as in the case of his contemporaries of the Schoenberg school, is almost omnipresent. Much Bach can sound sombre too.

Bach and Bartok were, surely, composing, not improvising on to a score. Their originality, as an aspect of their integrity, cannot have been other than spontaneous, though distilled through highly sensitive musical intellects.

Consider, for comparison, the admiration expressed for the simplicity, clarity, expressiveness and artlessness of children's art. However hard the child may be expected to *try* to paint like a trained adult, up to an age of about eleven many children are able to paint, in what is regarded as a childish mode, spontaneously. Sometimes they seem able *only* to paint with a spontaneity which is invariably lost shortly after that age. It is as if a child's vision, a way of looking at and perceiving the world, suddenly alters at that age. Thereafter the mind's reaction with the visually perceived world and the world of the imagination changes and what is painted in succeeding years reflects another set of visual values and, to interact with the visible world and the manifestations of the invisible self, a different psychological posture. Artists sometimes strive to recover the child's lost outlook – Dubuffet, for example. Very few succeed and I am not sure that they can be envied if they do. Alfred Wallis, a 'primitive' painter of sailing ships at sea, and treated rather like a mascot of the St Ives group of artists, seemed to see as simply as a child the limited subject-matter of his small pictures. But only if his range had been more extensive would it have been possible – perhaps – to judge his spontaneity. Among highly skilled twentieth-century artists whom I particularly admire for their ability to convey a sense of spontaneity, I would mention Paul Klee and Stanley Spencer. Each has a quirky sense of humour, sophisticated yet somehow innocent, conveying an unshakable humanity and an outlook simultaneously down-to-earth and out-of-this-world.

Yet spontaneity and either sophistication or a lack of it are not to be equated: they refer to different spheres of influence upon an artist's inspiration – 'contrived' may, in this context, be the opposite of 'spontaneous', whereas 'sophistication' concerns the style, though not the quality, of art.

There is one British artist whose paintings – all that I have seen – were childlike in the sense I am seeking to describe. Perhaps he had discovered how to *make* them so. In that case they were not, as they seemed, spontaneous. We may never know. I am referring to Roger Hilton, the last years of whose life, when the spirit was in him, suggest that the adult mind must mature and lose the vision of a child or fail to cope in the world of adult society.

Playing a musical instrument with the range of sensitivity of a violin to a soloist's standard is not for the weekend fiddler. A Sunday painter may show with professional artists – and sometime show them up. But without a technique which can only be acquired with years of daily practice, hours and hours of concentrated work, a musician will seldom have enough to sacrifice, *to journey away from*, to be able to approach spontaneity in the sense in which I am assuming Menuhin used that word.

Listening to Menuhin and Grappelli playing together on issued records of hits and evergreen melodies of the twenties and thirties, with jazz solos and choruses, I am not myself able to distinguish between the degree of spontaneity achieved by either. It may be that Menuhin's reactions are so swift as to sound as if they must be spontaneous when they are not; and Grappelli may, years ago, have developed a different skill, so as to contrive a simulation of spontaneity crystallized for perpetual presentation. On the sleeve-note to one of these commercially successful records reference is made to the contribution of a group of Dutch woodwind players, mainly from symphony orchestras, whose 'enthusiasm and enjoyment was obvious as the recording proceeded, and quite often there was an involuntary round of applause for the two soloists'. Unfortunately the enthusiastic atmosphere is not, for me, conveyed in the recorded music-making itself. As a cabaret act, with the sound supplemented by the sight of two musicians so dedicated to giving and receiving pleasure through performance, combining and sparking each other off, the delight of a dialogue-duet could be caught. But nothing of this reached me as I listened to these records.

So we have the sleeve-note to tell of the accompanying musicians' 'involuntary' applause, which I take to mean spontaneous, from the heart rather than the head. We can only speculate whether Menuhin approved the sleeve-note if he didn't write it. I wonder, in a rather cerebral way, if I might be wise to embark on a journey to spontaneity myself – if I knew how to set about it.

There is, however, a curious paradox in an aim to be spontaneous. It is implicit in this question: How can I pursue a journey to anything unless I do so deliberately? Menuhin says of a journey towards spontaneity '. . . the desire to travel that path was always latent; probably it is for other violinists'. Certainly one can wish for something to happen, a happy accident, an unsolicited phone call, a welcome invitation. But to wish for a change to take place in oneself involves a desire of a different order because, if it is not mere bullshit, it implies that one believes one can do something about it here and now. Now! Indeed, when else?

A whole journey cannot, of course, be made 'now'. But a spontaneous wish – and what can any wish be but spontaneous? – can initiate a self-propelled journey. And such a journey of inner transformation neither requires nor in practical terms entails relentless movement. If embarked upon with the right quality of determination and a desire which is intense yet free of worldly selfishness and demand or expectation of reward, such a transformation will continue in its own way and time. An aim made with integrity and single-mindedness, will enable one to reinforce the inner work set in motion and which persists without need for conscious intervention, much like the function of digestion initiated whenever we eat anything. The quality of will motivating such an aim overcomes the natural reaction of the rational mind, doubting, arguing and resisting any desire for change as unnecessary and dangerous.

So it seems that a special meaning has to be attributed to the intention to follow a journey to spontaneity. That intention might be expected itself to be spontaneous, though, as I have suggested, its implementation might require some degree of deliberate, non-spontaneous inner and outer work. I am fascinated to learn that for Menuhin 'the desire to travel that path was always latent' and that he believes this to be true also of other violinists. Other instrumentalists? Actors? And creative artists in any media? What if latent in *everyone* is a creative artist? Can professionals be creative? Status – amateur or professional – is not the point. Without a standard of technique, creativity lacks a vehicle adequate for the fulfilment of its potential; but in developing a high technical standard energy is in danger of being deflected from the service of creativity, and aim may be deflected to creativity from openness to spontaneity.

Most people in our kind of culture seem to take more naturally to some activities than to others, yet the child prodigy in any field seems to be comparatively rare. Even Menuhin, a prime example, had to learn technique and interpretive alternatives from others, few of whom (but Enesco for one) could approach his genius as an interpretive artist or, ultimately, as a teacher. Menuhin, like everyone else, acquired an overlay of know-how and conditioning which, as it accumulates over the years, is taken for granted, functions habitually and must form an ever-thickening insulation between spontaneity and actual output.

In the last chapter of *Unfinished Journey*, Menuhin describes briefly how he approaches, with discretion and understanding, the young violinists who come to the school he established at Stoke d'Abernon in 1964. He writes of trying above all 'to impart a sense of fluency, economy and precision in motion'. He emphasizes the basic importance of co-ordination of the hands, for which he invented exercises, and breathing exercises which are mysteriously 'planned to counter bias in favour of one particular co-ordination, and bring to consciousness the links in the chain of movement'. He adds:

> Intuition is born, I think, of many things happening at the same time but not quite simultaneously. Our reason is geared to taking one problem on its own, analysing it, and reaching a conclusion about how we shall proceed. But when we are faced with ten different factors, all acting upon each other and among them creating some astronomical total of variables, reason is defeated and only intuition can cope. Thus it is in violin playing – too much going on for direction by the conscious mind. In teaching, therefore, one can go only so far: one can prepare the ground, loosen the muscles, strengthen the fingers, point out all the elements to be co-ordinated so that any combination of movements may be made at any time. Then the player's vision takes over, intuitively selecting from those billions of possibilities the thousands it needs.

All that split-second co-ordination! There is not only 'too much going on for direction by the conscious mind' but it goes on far too quickly for meaningful intervention by the thinking part of that mind. As I enter into a technically flawful practice of the 'Giga' movement of Bach's second partita for violin I am at the same time drawn and driven by the *spirit* of the music. At my next lesson my teacher, a professional of the old Russo-Jewish school – no pad between instrument and shoulder to blanket resonance! – who is a perfectionist with due reverence for Bach and a slight over-reverence for Heifetz – nearly weeps at my faulty intonation. He begs me to practise slowly *and always in tune*, not playing the easier phrases faster and the harder ones slower, and to practise scales every day; and I know he is right. But I am carried away by the music's spirit working in my spirit. I don't know about spontaneity, in this context, but I know what I like to feel when I'm having a go.

The practice of painting has a special relevance here to our existence as creatures of time, who are nevertheless grossly ignorant of our relationship with it. In contrast to the interpretive musician, a painter may, as a rule, take what time he pleases on any particular picture. Subject always to the influences of his conditioning, he may decide 'spontaneously' whether to stop and declare a painting finished, to alter it radically or just to touch it up here or there. We are fortunate to be able to understand the effects of such alternative possibilities in some works of John Constable, where we can compare completed sketches of considerable sophistication to finished paintings of the same subjects. In his paintings of *The Hay Wain* the results of his choices are impressive. However, to each example we may legitimately apply Menuhin's words worth quoting again in this different context: '. . . when we are faced with ten different factors, all acting upon each other and among them creating some astronomical total of variables, reason is defeated and only intuition can cope . . . the [artist's] vision takes over, intuitively selecting from those billions of possibilities the thousands it needs.'

Perhaps Menuhin is implying that intuition is significantly distinguishable from spontaneity. Like Constable, Menuhin and any of those other violinists whom he would expect to share his latent desire to travel the path to spontaneity, must face the monumental task of side-stepping the burden of conditioning. It is precisely their training, above all to co-ordinate ear and necessarily involved muscles in the case of musicians and, in the case of painters, eye and hand which represents the negative task, the struggle to find a way on to a path towards spontaneity. In reality the task is completely different in kind and involves no struggle. At any and potentially every point along the path itself the very goal, the experience of spontaneity may arise if there is a strong enough aim to be open to it. Spontaneity cannot be harnessed but being open to it may become as natural as a bit between the teeth for a horse.

A film made of the artist John Hoyland, coinciding with the opening of a retrospective of his work, was televised on BBC2. He was described as 'reckoned by many both here and abroad to be this country's finest abstract painter. A key figure for younger artists, he has been both loved and hated to excess.' He was shown in the film starting a new painting on a huge, square canvas, explaining 'why, in bleaker moments, painting can seem "like flicking away in a corner with a feather duster" '. My notes of what he said are not to be relied on as in all instances verbatim but I trust I have not materially distorted his meaning.

Early in the film Hoyland spoke of his use of music – I think he called it 'rubbishy music' or something like that – to act as a sort of filter for the mind against working too consciously, adding with a throwaway laugh 'plus it stops you feeling so lonely'. For those of us who prefer to work to music if the alternative is silence, that seemed to express the value of background music corresponding closely to my own experience.

I jotted down phrases relevant to my theme, while watching Hoyland using with controlled strokes a wide brush, painting in bright oil colours put on so wet that they ran freely down the canvas. The artist would sometimes turn the canvas ninety or one hundred and eighty degrees so that the running paint would change direction – and the evolving painting take on a quite different appearance. Frequently he would with equal confidence – and equal diffidence – paint fresh colours over those previously applied with apparent abandon so far as concerned shapes on the canvas and the 'design' as a whole. I noted the following remarks:

'I don't think anything is random at all in the end . . . the absurdity of talking about it . . . one should't talk about it.'
'What's wrong with being self-indulgent?'

'. . . hours spent looking at it trying to decide what to do . . .'

On choosing colours he mentioned the excitement which he might experience from the application of a particular colour on one occasion, adding 'another time it would repulse me'; and 'I sometimes think I know too much about colour. I don't know enough, but . . .'

'I'll throw in something to try to surprise myself.'

'Everything's a danger – you know, getting it fiddly . . . a tightrope between becoming too fiddly and everything coming together . . . you've got to exercise some control . . .'

'I want to make simple paintings . . . maybe I've got to go through this complexity . . .'

Hoyland's response to the inquisition about his way of working (questions inaudible to viewers were asked to him during the filming) deserves close attention, but first I would refer to certain aspects of the work of an artist of unsurpassed significance in the history of Western art – Rembrandt. The series of his painting which has for many years captivated my interest is his self-portraits. He died aged sixty-three in 1669, leaving a sequence of self-portraits, some forty drawings and over sixty in oil, almost all of them of outstanding quality *as portraits*, each conveying an impression of the essence of his state of mind, not merely of his appearance at a particular time.

In 1982 a book I had long awaited was published devoted to the reproduction of all Rembrandt's self-portraits.[2] It recorded historically attested events in his life around the time when it is known or believed each self-portrait was painted. Rembrandt's moods and aspirations are there for one to read in the paintings themselves according to the degree of purity and profundity of one's own self-knowledge.[3]

Rembrandt did not need to paint himself over and over again as an exercise in portraiture for the last forty years of his life. He is said virtually to have kept himself on commissioned portraits in his middle years, and nearly one third of his creative output in oil paintings were portraits so it seemed he didn't lack for models. He often dressed up to paint himself, in one instance as the Apostle Paul. From his earliest self-portrait of about 1629 until his death, he drew and painted himself repeatedly. As an artist he seemed to reach in himself, almost invariably, an objectivity which would be remarkable in any portraitist

119

but is certainly unequalled in any self-portraitist. By means of this exceptional objectivity he could depict himself as he knew himself to be with a compassion which can only have stemmed from self-knowledge. It is easy to claim one's imagined strengths as 'one's own', but the weaknesses are more often projected – noticed in others rather than in oneself. Evidenced by his self-portraits, Rembrandt *knew*, from the age of about twenty-three, what it was to be a human being. He had no need to rely on descriptions, assessments and judgements of others on the subject. He illustrated this all-embracing understanding of the human condition especially in his last self-portraits, gripping and haunting as they are and completely without flamboyance, self-justification or cynicism. Evoked by his transparent and opaque brush-work is the spectrum of experience from triumph to tragedy, from delight to remorse, from confidence to resignation.

This digression into the mid-seventeenth century has a peculiar relevance to the meaning and significance of spontaneity in music. To be so 'inside' oneself and yet detached as to be able to portray the perceived truth with Rembrandt's objectivity is a gift earned only by 'Zen' masters, from whatever religion they seek truth through direct apprehension. That others have approached a similar degree of objectivity in an exceptional single self-portrait I would accept. Names come to mind but I am almost invariably disappointed when I return to look into the eyes of other great artists, through their self-portraits, to find only a view of superficialities and composed or ephemeral expressions.

Back, then, to Hoyland about whose manner of painting – it looked like inspired doodling and had, incidentally, changed radically to much smaller and more controlled pictures, by 1985 – it is too easy to be churlishly dismissive. An admirer of his work, John McEwen, contributed an essay in the illustrated catalogue to Hoyland's second London retrospective, sponsored by the Arts Council at the Serpentine Gallery in October 1979. In describing Hoyland's development to that point, he wrote that his paintings become:

> increasingly symphonic, increasingly to look as if they have been built [in the medium of colour] . . . Impact of scale, colour and texture may initially disguise the logical and progressively complex evolution of these works, and their correspondingly studied attention to detail: the precise compositional balance, the manipulation of

ever more difficult, sometimes downright outrageous, colour sequences. That they invariably express emotional force and physical freedom is the most telling tribute to Hoyland's skill. Not one of those specks of colour, even in the most mistily atmospheric pictures of his New York City period, is unconsidered. As he strives for a fuller – the fullest possible – range of plastic effect, he becomes more and more deliberate. How do you structure a painting? How do you get paint in, on and across a surface? How do you make form unsymbolic? How can you encourage the possibility of a lucky accident without an equivalent loss of control? How can you achieve all these things and still retain a sense of spontaneity?

We may sympathize with McEwen in his attempt to discharge his commission (or self-imposed task) to write about Hoyland's work, which he obviously admires. Yet we may feel more sympathy for Hoyland. He, however, may ignore our sympathy and prefer McEwen's instructive examination of the creative process by which his striking paintings are produced. In my own years as a painter I painted a number of abstracts in much the same way as Hoyland paints his. Most of mine were on a more modest scale and I painted from the therapeutic need to express myself through painting combined with the vanity of a natural show-off. What I lacked, and admired in others as I do now in Hoyland, is style – an individual, characteristic and consistent style capable, for instance, of giving spontaneous pleasure to people who like looking at colourful paintings.

Unless Hoyland would urgently dissociate himself from the association, I would claim for him, as for myself when I was painting 'inspired' doodles, no more spontaneity than an artist may allow spontaneity to dictate, in a non-abstract painting, his whole design and every brush-stroke. That is not to say that *any* such painting may not 'still retain a sense of spontaneity' – or at least convey such a sense – though the sense itself may have been contrived. There is a hint here of a possible approach to a valid definition of genius.

Hoyland's own words, which I have summarized, uncannily reflect my own experience of painting with controlled abandon. One of the most revealing remarks he made of the process of trial and error was, 'I'll throw in something to try to surprise myself.' In such a gesture there may be spontaneity: but first a specific pattern or design must be established, and be discernible, into or against which a surprise element may be thrown. The artist's aim is 'to try to surprise' himself; the onlooker or anyone seeing the painting subsequently in its 'finished' form may be incapable of surprise at any particular feature in it. But for the artist and perhaps for the artist alone the surprise element may provide a focus in the picture for which the rest, previously 'important' in itself, will thenceforth be a background or frame, to reinforce or set in contrast the new point which attracts primary attention. The artist may then be pleased, for good reason. One looks at the picture struck by the incongruity or the unexpected rightness in its context of the surprise object, shape, colour splash or whatever it is. That makes a good contemporary picture of a certain kind; another kind, of the 'minimal' rather than the 'kitchen sink' school, succeeds, if at all, by the impressiveness of its consistency, by one's astonishment that there is absolutely nothing surprising in it.

As I mentioned earlier, the performance of any but the most unconventional modern work of music entails a recognized time scale which is, within fairly close limits, preordained by the composer's indications or the improviser's self-discipline. A performance of any work lasting more than an hour strains the concentration of a solo instrumentalist and any audience but, whatever the length of the work, if it is worth hearing it is worth the effort needed to listen to it all with attention. In contrast the painting which may be completed in four hours or as many years is perceived by its audience in an instant. It may take longer to absorb details and inter-relationships, but it is all there at every moment and its features may be approached in any order and from any angle, whereas we can perceive a musical work only in real-time, sequentially. This difference is significant because it highlights the distinction between spontaneity in the creative acts of the artist and the composer; and in the effects on the audiences respectively of a painting and the performance of a musical composition.

Can anything 'thrown in as a surprise' – a surprise even to the thrower – be a product of spontaneity? It presupposes either a decision to throw in something unexpected or an unexpected decision to throw in something. There is an implied calculation or realization of what is right, natural, to be expected which alone rules out spontaneity. For a creative artist under the influence of inspiration, the elements of motive and decision are absent, hence 'spontaneity'. Even an

122

unconscious motive – to 'show them'! – renders spontaneity impossible or deceptive.

Decisions, and the intellectual and emotional motives which underlie them, may be violent just as they may be gentle, or anywhere on a scale between. Anger can motivate a sudden act. Such an act may include a stroke, no doubt a violent stroke, with a paintbrush. Because of the speed of its application it is easily confused with spontaneity. A tune and rhythm 'spontaneously' played by a violinist might be in a fast or a slow tempo; or should spontaneous music-making be only in a fast tempo? Is there room in the mind, then, for a *decision* to 'throw in a surprise'? And is there also room for an attitude of not caring what happens, what the effect is of trying anything which either chance or one's conditioning might introduce? In spontaneity there has to be freedom – from decision-making and motive – and a corresponding feeling of inevitability perhaps accompanied by joy. No wonder Menuhin wishes to journey to it.

'Spontaneous activity' is what I have described in terms of painting and playing the violin. From a listener's point of view there can be a spontaneous wish to listen to *some*, possibly any, music – unless that wish is already an habitual decision. A choice of what to listen to presupposes a knowledge of what is available from which to make the choice.

Spontaneous activity can only spring from a part of consciousness disengaged from conditioning, while spontaneous passivity, akin to apathy, provides neither satisfaction for instinctive needs such as food nor luxuries or entertainment which are objects of conditioned expectation and appetites. 'Spontaneous passivity' is generally enforced by weariness, physical, mental or emotional. To listen to music a degree of emotional engagement is desirable – one should *want* to hear it, even if only as background. In a state of 'spontaneous passivity' one is emotionally 'wrung out'; and then no music can make any impact on one unless to invoke such a feeling of desperation by even its minimal demand on one, as to impel some action to effect immediate escape from it.

There is also a state of 'spontaneous inactivity', (something quite different from spontaneous passivity) when, for no apparent reason, one suddenly finds oneself able to perceive incoming sense-impressions for what they are, uncensored and uninterpreted by prejudices, preconceptions or, in short, by the filter of one's conditioning. As there is no impairment of relevant energies to detract from the rare best-of-one's-attention, the resulting experience is pure and makes an exceptional impact on one's consciousness.

By practices akin to some of those recommended for meditation it is possible to achieve deliberately the kind of inactivity I have just described, that is to achieve it otherwise than spontaneously. But this is a book about some of the uses of music. It is not about the 'uses of meditation' – which contradiction in terms I find at once outrageous and hilarious. We have discussed purposes for which music may be used. And who 'uses' music as a sense-orientated stimulus for any of those purposes is a meaningful question, whereas to speak of anyone who would 'use' meditation is to misunderstand the function and potential of that internal *state*. Nevertheless the practices of relevance can be studied and their operation triggered by the switching of attention from left to right hemispheres of the brain. Hence the question '*who* uses music?' may after all be asked relevantly in relation to the quite different functioning of the two sides of the brain.[4]

---

[1] From a lecture quoted by the Rev. Paul Oestreicher; *The Penguin Dictionary of Modern Quotations* (Revised edition, 1980) quotes a variation from Barth's obituary in the *New York Times* of 11 December 1968: 'Whether the angels play only Bach in praising God I am not quite sure: I am sure, however, that *en famille* they play Mozart.'
[2] *Rembrandt: Self Portraits* by Christopher Wright, Gordon Fraser, 1982.
[3] See the author's monograph *Rembrandt and Angels*, Institute for Cultural Research, 1982.
[4] See *The Psychology of Consciousness* by Robert Ornstein, W. H. Freeman & Co., San Francisco, 1972.

11
FOR EVER NEW MUSIC

Soon after my return to civilian life after nearly seven years in the army, from 1939 to 1946, while I was a nearly middle-aged law student, I began to explore a new world of music by monthly attendance at concerts given by the Committee, now the Society for the Promotion of New Music – the SPNM. In those days it was impolitely known as 'The Commotion'. It was founded in 1943 by a conductor and composer Francis Chagrin, a Rumanian-born immigrant to England. He realized the frustration of student composers who had little or no opportunity to hear their works performed and, consequently, lacked a vital dimension in the development of their creative potentialities. For comparison, how could painters develop if *their* compositions could be the subject of verbal description only and were never *seen*?

On not very comfortable chairs in a square recital room with appalling acoustics over the shop of Augeners, music publishers of Marlborough Street, I used to sit under one of several windows with stained-glass portraits of 'great' nineteenth-century composers. My chosen window portrayed a namesake, perhaps an ancestor of mine, Anton no doubt rather than his brother Nikolai Rubinstein. The music we heard was of very variable standards, but mostly reasonably well played. Afterwards the wretched composers suffered or enjoyed a discussion by sympathetic and not so sympathetic fellow composers and amateur listeners like me, following a professional appraisal.

Many of them were at pains to explain that we had heard only an early student work composed months or years before; more recent compositions were in an entirely different style. I often wondered – would it be in the composer's 'own' style?

At a not quite typical, unusually prolonged discussion after one of these recitals the audience analysed the music for evidence of the appropriateness of the title of a piece – a trio with a part for double bass, played by Francis Baines, I think – *The Goose in the Garage*. The composer listened patiently until the chairman for the evening asked him to comment. 'Oh,' he said, deadpan, 'the title has nothing to do with the music: on the day I finished composing it there just happened to be a goose in my garage.'

The SPNM has since enhanced its search for means to 'promote new music' in the best interests of composers who are British, or work in the British Isles. It received an endowment, unusual for a charity with such musically esoteric objects, under the will of an elderly Armenian recluse, Arthur Paul, whom I used to visit on behalf of the society at his home in a large house in Frognal. He occupied only his bedroom where he lived in a dressing-gown on his bed under which he kept an old pair of black army boots. He was surrounded by piles of 78s which I am sure he never played, and by stacks of books found, on his death, to consist mainly of soft 'porn'; he had not looked at it for a long time, to judge by the dust on them. He evidently felt himself a composer manqué – hence his residuary bequest of a not inconsiderable estate to the society of whose existence and financial need he had heard from Alexander Goehr.

The bequest had been provisionally valued at well over £150,000. As one of Arthur Paul's executors, with his own solicitor and his bank, I gave this news to Francis Chagrin and the then secretary of the society, John Woolf, and was invited to report it to the next meeting of the executive committee. When I had made my announcement there was a stunned silence. Then a timid voice from down the table asked 'Does that mean that I can hire the drums for our next concert?' It did.

For many months after that money – whether to save it or how much to spend and how to spend it – was discussed more often, for longer and with more heat than was music. But the best application of income *for the most effective promotion of new music*, with occasional brave forays into captial, was and still is a vital issue in all the society's deliberations.

What is so different about this age that new music should need to be promoted nowadays as it did not formerly? There is much more of it about, composed in a far wider variety of styles than hitherto, to be played, to be heard, to be criticized. It is arguable that this should reduce rather than increase the need for its promotion. But little of the much-more-of-it is technically, even when it is literally, 'new music'. Yet it is not the object cᶠ the SPNM and it is no obsession of mine to rate technical novelty higher than creative *musical* originality, combined with a quality of craftsmanship beyond mere competence. Of *course* one is always on the lookout for genius. It's as simple as that! And even the music of a genius needs to be performed and heard for a first time.

On the subject of creative genius the paradoxes are formidable. We can never be sure that the artist starving in an attic would have produced better – or as good – work at the same stage in his career on a generous patron's grant, in a custom-built studio. He would not have been the same person.

Would Mozart have composed 'better' had he taken the trouble to labour over his music after writing it down? Or Brahms had he composed 'in a flash' with such confidence in his first inspiration that he would not alter a note once he had produced a written score? The questions are meaningless. Mozart composed like that and Brahms like *that*. For neither of them could it have been otherwise.

It is not a question of seeking to nurture young composers artificially. Make composer A listen to more seventeenth-century music, and nothing else; let composer B live in a superbly equipped electronic studio for six months with no material worries; leave composer C in the squalor of his bigamous family muddle and give his 'wives' his scholarship money. All such contrived schemes are doomed to failure. Because we cannot comprehend 'ideal' aims we cannot apply 'appropriate' means.

I am deliberately encroaching upon the field of Deryck Cooke in *The Language of Music* when I enquire what are the *psychological* influences on one or another of the compositions of a composer and on one or another composer. Was that goose in the garage irrelevant after all to the music composed when a goose was stuck in the garage? The products of the creative process seem to come from a part of a mind quite distinct from that part which interrelates with the environment by reacting emotionally, intellectually and physically to the stimulus of sense-perceptions.

Composers do what they have to do at one end of the tunnel of created music; but look at what is happening at the other end. Members of a critical audience including a number of practising musicians listen with a special attention, because a programme-type title has been given to a musical work which they cannot have heard before, for which no programme notes have been supplied. It later transpires they have been listening for expected events in the course of the music and interpreting incidents of only an abstract musical origin to fit a programmatic circumstance which, the composer eventually assures them, is completely irrelevant to those incidents.

Nevertheless by the very act of looking out for things that may not have been there we, the listeners to the performance, may have heard what we would otherwise have missed in terms of the composer's *intentions*, because we gave unaccustomed attention to the music itself. Alternatively we may have distorted the structure of that music in our own minds by trying to fit it into the anticipated patterns of sound evoked by the dramatic title. When a work is given a title apt to a programme which corresponds to the music – for example Berlioz' *Symphonie Fantastique* or Elgar's symphonic study *Falstaff* – a search for the story-line may distract the listener from the music itself; or it may channel attention into aural representations of events and so help the listener's concentration.

Contemporary composers are no more and no less involved with listeners' image-making than were composers of former days. Who would demand of a composer of genius that he should score music so that every listener to it will experience only what the composer intended? Never mind what he intends, does any composer expect any work to be listened to as pure sound only? Or pure visual imagery? Or a precise, unique programme? The composer is, after all, appealing for the attention of listeners which may seem to be freely available but has nevertheless to be caught. And anyway the idea of freedom of attention is largely illusory. So free is it that it is virtually out of the control even of the individual listeners themselves.

Why does anyone listen to music who is not capable of and willing to listen always with constant directed attention? Because, surely, we expect to derive pleasure of one kind or another from music which we have chosen to listen to; for certain benefits attention to the music is unnecessary. Indeed some kinds of pleasure and some benefits would not occur to a listener following every phrase, every note, every nuance with dedication. These considerations have special relevance to the problems of promoting new music.

One obvious issue is that through the use of unfamiliar, perhaps never before exploited, sound combinations and timbres some new music is found 'difficult' to listen to. It gives none of those pleasures to be experienced in easier, familiar forms and musical sounds. We are, perhaps, sated with more familiar music, longing to have our receptive inclinations titillated by fresh sounds and patterns of sound. Then music that does not seem immediately attractive may be tolerated, not to give it the benefit of the doubt but to find out whether familiarity will disclose virtues and felicities which were not immediately apparent.

New music may strike a first-time listener as monotonous and boring. The great *Adagio* movement in Beethoven's A minor string quartet Op.132 (*Heiliger Dankesang eines Genesenen an die Gottheit, in der lydischen Tonart* – a hymn in the Lydian mode of thanksgiving to God for recovery from illness) may have seemed like that when first performed; or Stravinsky's *Les Noces*, or the *Chaconne* in Britten's second string quartet. Later each of these works can be appreciated as among the masterpieces of their creators. Other works, even by great composers, may seem not really worth listening to over and over again in spite of their high acclaim. For example, I find myself enjoying Schubert's *Trout* quintet less and less at every hearing – it is certainly charming but lacks that intellectual element which compels me to follow and revel in his last string quartet, the G major, Op.161.

It is easy to forget that composers who extend the range of musical expression in new directions may know no better than their first audiences what will last, indeed what will ever be played again. The composer is compelled by the dictates of creative forces within him to compose, and to compose in the way he does: some are barely restrained by practicalities of performance. All this activity should not be, indeed it cannot effectively be discouraged. Even those who consider that no music worth listening to was composed after the nineteenth century, or after Debussy or some other random deadline[1] may in a less dogmatic mood concede that it would be irrational and indeed uncivilized not to encourage the production of new and therefore inevitably sometimes experimental compositions.

The experimental essays of practitioners in the visual arts are, on completion, immediately available to be appreciated, condemned, laughed at or puzzled over by anyone who cares to look. Then, given acceptable lighting and a sight-path between bobbing champagne glasses at the private view, nothing intervenes between artist and art-lover/critic. The composer, however, cannot offer the end-product of his creative talent without the mediation of performance. Unless he can perform his new composition himself, to his own satisfaction, he is generally at the mercy of friends who may fail to match the inspiration with which he credits himself.

It is a wonder that any young composers survive the discouragement inherent in the practice of their craft. But it is no wonder that only an infinitesimal part of the laborious output of composers will be played more than once if it is performed at all. Is it enough to rely on luck or fate to ensure the survival of the fittest composers and the promotion of the worthiest compositions? We shall never know. Is it generally the pushy, the facile and the sycophants who get away with it, while composers of integrity, modest or at least reticent and maybe deserving – are neglected?

The SPNM at least gives composers in the latter category a chance to hear and to have heard by others what poring over their own scores will never tell them – how the new composition actually sounds, whether for performers, for audience and for the composer himself 'it works'. Hence the categories into which I have crudely divided composers – those who 'get away with it' and those neglected into oblivion – are, however, artificial and therefore irrelevant. For the inexperienced composer, to hear his early, for him experimental, music performed and to recognize its limitations and its potentialities through the reactions of performers and audience is essential if his creative talent is to mature. That is one elementary way that the SPNM seeks to fulfil its object to promote new music. Concerts and recitals 'only' have to be organized and a relatively small audience will suffice for that purpose.

So long as works suitable for performance in spite of any lack of style or polish are selected conscientiously by members of reading panels and there are funds to enable a diligent administration to build programmes round the appropriate performers and to put on the concerts, the composers whose works are chosen are well served. The whole operation is so complex that several years may elapse from the completion of the scoring of a work to first public performance even through the auspices of the SPNM. By the time it is heard its composer may be writing quite differently and claim to have little or no use for the lessons which he might originally have absorbed. Prompt performance even of selected works is seldom practicable. For all the disappointments and frustrations much benefit has however been conferred on very many composers who give unstinted support to the SPNM later, when they are successful and honoured.

There are competitions for composers as there are for performers. But works of art, unlike industrial products, are not mutually exclusive. Such consumer-orientated concepts as 'Best Buy' or 'Worth Considering' do not apply to original works of art. Fortunately there is no monopoly of merit or, *pace* the wits, critical profundity. An American writer, Bill Nye (1850–96), is quoted as commenting 'Wagner's music is better than it sounds.' Probably Mark Twain, or it may have been Lord Goodman, improved on this, with 'Wagner's music is not as bad as it sounds.'

In the seventeenth and eighteenth centuries much of the then new music which has survived was promoted by the support of wealthy patrons who provided their protégés not only with a livelihood but with performers and audiences too. There is no reason why the court assembled at the behest of an archduke should have appreciated the *avant garde* fare proffered by the house composer. But we may be right to assume that they generally did so, since so little of the music of second- and third-rate composers is played these days though much more of their music was probably played at the time than that of the handful of composers we now recognize as first-rate. An occasional airing of hack works by superficially inspired composers confirms the superiority of the few great ones among their contemporaries.

An idea that it is a pity we cannot encourage only the really good composers and persuade the others to find other outlets for their energies would be utterly misguided. To excel at anything presupposes the existence of the less than so excellent, of all degrees. In the creative arts, a range of practitioners striving, irrespective of merit and prospects, can essentially provide the most understanding as well as the most critical audiences and contribute to the milieu in which the creatively talented may be recognized and best appreciated. Besides, posterity may take a different view of relative merits.

That is reason enough to seek to promote good new music by encouraging an enthusiasm for the composition of new music, almost whatever its quality. Anyone with the interest and the ear to tackle the sheer drudgery of composing *may* hide an unexpected talent. In an atmosphere of enthusiasm for new music of all kinds it is more likely that a genius will emerge than from a cultural vacuum.

Nevertheless, because of the nature of the craft, amateurs are less likely to flock to evening classes in composition than in the case of painting. In music amateur practitioners find their challenge and their individual and corporate pleasures in performing. And why should they tackle modern music when there is a huge repertoire of works which are enjoyable to play and to hear, from the easy to the not so easy to perform?

Just as composers of every standard as well as style should be given encouragement for the successful promotion of 'new music', so for the same purpose should new music *not* be promoted at the expense of the music of earlier periods. Of course as time – for practice, for concert-going, for listening – is inevitably limited so time is spent on music of one period at the expense, it may seem, of music of all other periods. But the time measure is not clock time but the time of the musical mind whose scope for expansion in terms of experience is wide enough to be regarded as tending to the infinite.

Of course, the artificial promotion of any particular period or style of music would be bound to reinforce the impact of fashion already recognized in relation to styles of performance. Purity may be contrasted with expressiveness, for example. Playing Bach's six sonatas and partitas for solo violin Heifetz may be regarded as a supreme master in the former category; his intonation is invariably impeccable, as my violin teacher, Ivan Aarons, never ceases to remind me, and the purity of his interpretation is incomparable. But I find it also, on occasion, unsatisfying – not because of its 'perfection' – that word has no meaning for me in relation to musical performance – but because I sometimes seek a subtler expressiveness as may be found in a more recent recording by Oscar Shumsky. In the same works of Bach, I have, however, come to prefer the performances on record of an Israeli of Rumanian origin, Sergiu Luca, playing on a Baroque violin, an unusual Nicolo Amati, restored, as the note in the box has it 'to approximate its seventeenth-century condition and adjustment' – about half a tone lower than today's concert pitch. The result, in terms of musical experience, is a revelation of warmth and expressiveness *without* divergence from classical purity of style. And later, in 1984, I was overwhelmed again as soon as I heard the recording of the same works by Sigiswald Kuijken, a Belgian playing on a violin made about 1700 by Giovanni Grancino in Milan. Like Luca's instrument this is said to have been restored to its original Baroque condition so far as possible. And Kuijken uses neither shoulder support nor chin rest, holding the violin so that 'the chin never touches the instrument'. Never mind the technique, the performances are magical.

Musical life in this country seems at present healthy thanks, to an extraordinary but incalculable extent, to the influence on it over a period of about sixty years of Sir Robert Mayer, who was very widely mourned when he died aged 105 in 1985, and more recently of Sir William Glock and a host of individuals in the field of performing, conducting and composing. As I contemplated some names for a list of such individuals I realized that a professional orchestral player might not have the same respect for some of them as I have assumed from their public reputations boosted, it may be, by non-musical media consideration. Paradoxically the undeservedly popular figures may do more for the 'promotion of music' than some of their worthier colleagues. The promotion of 'serious' music since the end of the 1914–18 War has been a notable consequence of the excellence of radio programmes since the introduction of the Third Programme.

Within this excellence, however, fashions can undoubtedly be discerned, hence my concern that enthusiasm to propagate new music by stuffing it into the ears of a reluctant, even resistant public would be bound to be counter-productive as much for those inside as for those outside the existing music-listening community. Who can blame anyone for switching off who gets no pleasure, yet, from listening to music written and performed with strange instrumentations and in an unfamiliar style, which *seems* to make 'a horrible sound'?

No composer widely recognized as 'great' can have failed to extend the borders of previously familiar music. Some have done it with revolutionary effect, from Monteverdi to Wagner, from Beethoven to Bartok, from Schoenberg to Stockhausen. Others – Bach, Haydn,

133

Mozart, Debussy, Webern – have introduced their admirers more tactfully to the sounds and forms to be developed by their successors. When Mozart wrote his divertimento known as *A Musical Joke* (K.522) the deliberate wrong notes, the occasional coarse and inharmonious harmonies were accepted because he had defined them, in advance, as intended to amuse by their incongruity. The introductory bars of the last of his six string quartets dedicated to Haydn, that in C major (K.465), give it the nickname 'The Dissonant' or 'The Discord': his contemporaries are not known to have found them funny. Nor are they. They are like an object from the twentieth century transported backwards, as if by a time machine, and available for study some three hundred years before the music of the intervening years had prepared audiences to listen in a receptive mood to notes in close juxtaposition which were formerly regarded as 'false relations'.

No extent of familiarity, no number of extra repetitions can convert a discord into a concord, dissonance into assonance; beyond octaves, beyond the chords of fourths and fifths, dissonance is a matter of degree as fewer and fewer overtones coincide or blend in the ways we have been conditioned to find acceptable or agreeable. What is deemed inharmonious by one generation will sound positively – even if it is only relatively – harmonious to a later generation. The musical use to which relative disharmony may be put has no less bearing on the resultant music, and the way audiences will react to it, than the facts themselves of its construction in terms of harmony.

Is it inherent in atonal music to reflect *angst*, to sound as if it was composed in a state of deep depression? There may be exceptions, though I cannot think of any, but they would be unexpected. There would be likely to be an underlying sense of restlessness in the absence of a secure – or even an insecure – home to return to. Where there is no keynote, as it were, we do not know where we are or, therefore, where we are going; consequently we do not know, from the absence of such signposts as we have come to expect and to interpret reliably in the Western classical tradition, when we have arrived or, slightly in advance, when we are about to arrive. Indeed the message conveyed from the early bars of strictly atonal music must be that there is no 'arriving' in the piece because there is no particular (tonal) place to go to. If we find an atonal work, or a phrase in it, 'beautiful' it may be because of some passing affinity to a tonal tune or cadence or because we are so familiar with it that we 'feel at home with it' in spite of its own nomadic tonality.

Schoenberg tore himself out of the musical world of Wagner, Richard Strauss and Mahler through his own inner need to portray a mood for which the classical-romantic schools offered him no adequate means of expression. He is quoted as saying 'There is plenty more good music to be composed in the key of C major': he was not terminating an era by the adoption of his revolutionary structural device but he was freeing future generations from the power of historical conditioning which caught Hindemith, Reger, Zemlinsky and others in a backwater with no apparent outlet. Now, given the possible outlet of atonality, composers can choose to follow the former mainstream or the atonal school with such originality as they have at their command, or to mix the two (as indeed did Schoenberg in his later works), if not seeking yet newer means and modes of expression within a disciplined form.

That the rules of the tone-row which Schoenberg laid down for the framework of his own composition were strict is not surprising, if atonal music may rightly be regarded as the music of despair. Anyone inclined to compose under its discipline – that is, not doing so only experimentally – would, on the evidence of most of this music composed and performed to date, be less free than other people to regard the world otherwise than dolefully. In a gloomy state it does seem that we have less relative freedom to choose alternative moods or conduct. It is hard indeed to snap out of a depression, to overcome fear, or to cease to feel justifiably angry. Yet, no doubt in other, less negative states, atonality has been adopted to more cheerful effect as the mood-influence of Schoenberg is dissipated in the course of experimentation and by those free to express temperaments nurtured in quite different emotional environments.

For generations of music-lovers, familiar at least with music from the traditions of the great classical and romantic composers, Schoenberg's early atonal works, from *Pierrot Lunaire* onwards, sounded not only 'difficult' because of unfamiliarity with the idiom but, even after repeated hearings if these were tolerated, still disagreeable. Schoenberg's experiment might have been stillborn: his own closest disciples, Berg and Webern, nevertheless composed distinguished and expressive music which many have found not as unattractive as most of Schoenberg's own atonal music. That others have adopted the basic idiom, developed by Schoenberg himself into the 'twelve-note' technique, to the present day – from Stravinsky to Dallapicolla and Nono in Italy and Humphrey Searle and Elizabeth Lutyens in Great Britain, for example – and that the music of this school is still widely performed suggests incontravertibly that it has a continuing attraction for some composers and performers and, as significantly, for audiences, however superficially unpleasant a listener may find some of it even after hearing many excellent performances.

This surely suggests that such music fills a gap in the expressive range of the music of former times. From the pre-classical music, mostly for solo voice accompanied on the lute, of John Dowland (1563–1606), from the penultimate symphony, No.40 in G minor (K.550) by Mozart (1756–91), to the Viennese classics notably Haydn, Beethoven and Schubert, to the romantics, Tchaikovsky's sixth symphony, the *Pathétique*, and, in the twentieth century, Vaughan Williams' sixth symphony, the music of these successive eras could and did express extremes of grief, anxiety, despair and nothingness; but evidently some experience in the range and scale of human emotions remained to be expressed quite differently by the twelve-note school. Anyone may supply his own adjectives to describe his emotional reactions to examples of this musical idiom – my own suggestions would include rootless, self-pitying or without help.

In the final chapter of *The Language of Music*, on 'The Large-Scale Functioning of Musical Language', Deryck Cooke considers in some detail the elements in Mozart's fortieth and Vaughan Williams' sixth symphonies which establish the unities of their themes. Both, in their very different styles, are shown to be exceptional examples of music which audiences hear gladly though each expresses emotions generally recognized as unhappy or, in experience, unpleasant.

Cooke was concerned primarily with the vocabulary of the composers. He usefully provides a spring-board, as it were, for an examination of the emotions which may be invoked in members of audiences by various musical compositions. After investigating the language of music ultimately through a general analysis of the Mozart and Vaughan Williams symphonies, Cooke asks[3] 'is music only a language of the emotions, and nothing more?' He goes on:

In an age which views emotions with suspicion, some readers may well react strongly against the idea that music is concerned entirely with this dubious element in the human make-up. After all man has an intellect, a moral sense, and a metaphysical faculty which we call a spirit or a soul. Can music express nothing of these? . . . Although music is self-evidently incapable of expressing intellectual ideas . . . a vast amount of intellectual labour goes into producing any large-scale work and . . . miniatures are not the work of morons. To be a master of the musical art, on any scale, a man has to do a great deal of thinking as well as feeling, and the value of any first-rate work is at least half due to the technique which has realized the expressive intention with such mastery.

With regard to the moral sense, our question is half-answered. We have seen that, by vitalizing various basic terms expressing different emotions, and juxtaposing them in an ordered pattern, making some of them fundamental, persistent, and finally victorious, and others subsidiary, intermittent, and finally vanquished, a composer can express an unambiguous moral attitude towards life. The tremendously affirmative and inspiring impact of Beethoven's music [Cooke had referred earlier in particular to the *Eroica* symphony] arises from the fact that the positive emotions win through in the end, and that there is never any doubt that they are going to; the depressing effect of a work like Tchaikovsky's *Pathétique* symphony is due to the final establishing and emphasizing of the emotion of despair.[4] We need not feel ashamed that music should have a moral effect only by placing emotional moods in a significant order: psychology has shown that our whole life is propelled by these instinctive urges, and that it is by balancing and ordering them that we achieve a valuable, creative attitude to life.

Without necessarily accepting every detail of Cooke's argument, certain implications of his conclusion seem right. Following the passage quoted above, Cooke refers to his earlier observation that the painful emotions of Mozart's fortieth symphony 'are controlled and to some extent counter-balanced by rhythmic vitality and formal perfection . . . a lack of driving rhythm need not mean moral weakness at all, but only quiet meditation and serenity of mind; and sometimes it may mean that active, assertive life has been renounced in favour of other experiences felt to be of more value – transfiguration in death, for

137

example, as at the end of *Tristan*, or longing for the unattainable, as in much of the music of Delius. In such cases, the listener's own evaluation of the experience concerned (arising from his own attitude to life) will inevitably condition his moral reaction to the music.'

A listener's motives or reasons for choosing, where choice is possible, to listen to one work or to one performance of a work rather than to any other, may be appraised from useful pointers in both the passages quoted above. Perhaps, for other purposes, one would argue about what 'psychology has shown' or whether 'our whole life is propelled' by the 'instinctive urges' of 'emotional moods' which great composers place 'in a significant order'; and as to our ability to achieve 'a valuable, creative attitude to life' by 'balancing and ordering' these instinctive urges. But a sense of satisfaction about a particular musical work of any length and complexity does seem to derive from the apparent success of the composer in balancing and ordering the musical representations of emotional moods to achieve a valuable *created* representation of a self-consistent and so valid attitude to life.

What Cooke meant by 'a valuable creative attitude to life' I do not know; unless he intended to refer to an attitude to life valuable because it involves a composer in an artistically creative craft. In its context he would seem to have embraced all of humanity in relation to the achievement in question rather than only the creative artist in any medium. Cooke elsewhere[5] summarizes the creative act in music as a unity, 'the transformation of a complex of emotions into musical form – normally manifesting itself as a continuous process' of which he lists a number of overlapping stages from 'a complex of emotions within the composer's unconscious' which 'presses for an outlet – for expression, communication to others in musical form', to the complete work resulting from conscious craftsmanship interpenetrated and transformed at all stages by the unconscious 'creative imagination'. A performer, who should surely avoid public performance unless convinced of the work's unity in the sense described, may then effectively *recreate* the composer's representation of the particular complex of emotions transformed into musical form and embodied in it, inescapably contributing his own interpretation through his own corresponding complex of emotions. And the listener perceives, absorbs and re-interprets the same complex of emotions. To the extent that the details of one performance or another correspond with the details of a listener's emotional experience within that complex it will

138

satisfy him or at least convince him of its integrity.

There is no reason, therefore, why an unfamiliar work, a work on first hearing, should not in this sense satisfy a listener; or it may leave him uncertain of its complete 'success' or certain that no additional hearings would be justified if the listener seeks a feeling of satisfaction or, in sum, pleasure. Later, as a result, it may be, of emotional maturation or a performance of another quality, a listener may revise that earlier reaction, in either direction of course. Concerts provide an ideal setting for almost compulsory re-appraisal where any member of the audience may choose to go to hear particular performers or the performance of one or more of the works on the programme and so be obliged to sit and listen to others whose inclusion in the programme was not of itself attractive to him.

If a contemporary composer is not merely note-spinning to create an impression of originality or for purely experimental reasons there is no reason why music which appears difficult to listen to should not represent a complex of emotions true to his experience. And as interpreted in performance it may equally be found to correspond with a similar complex of emotions within the range of experience of members of an audience – a range not touched on let alone reached, perhaps, by any music they had previously heard.

Here is justification for the decision of some contemporary composers to leave to chance, to a far greater extent than must normally apply, the effect of their compositions in performance. John Cage, for example, abdicated much of a composer's customary ordering of the material of his composition in such a work as his *Imaginary Landscape*, first performed in 1951, for which a conductor guided the performers, two on each of twelve radio sets, to follow the ratio of sound to silence and dynamics laid down by the composer who can hardly be said to have taken responsibility for the resultant sounds in any performance. Leif Segerstam, however, has aimed at 'a utopian ideal which he calls the "organic musical kaleidoscope" '[6] involving improvisation within guidelines by a group of orchestral musicians playing together without a conductor. Stockhausen in his work *Cycle* (1959), for a single percussionist, left to the performer a choice on which page to begin and where, therefore, to end any particular performance. And in *The New Penguin Dictionary of Music*[7] Arthur Jacobs describes a 'moment' as a brief segment of a composition with its own musical characteristic, a structural concept in composition devised by Stockhausen where occurrences within each 'moment' may be held more important than the succession, which may be indeterminate, between moments, as in his 'Moments' for soprano, 4 choirs and 13 instruments (1964).

Of course there is no reason why a performance of such a work should not, as it happens, correspond sufficiently with a complex of emotions of any listener as to be valid for him at the time. It can thus satisfy some, probably unconscious, desire in him to have recreated in such musical form a representation, an interpretation, of that complex. In a traditional sense the work can hardly be said to have been composed; the 'composer' is not offering to the performers or listeners his own transformation into musical form of such a complex of emotions. He is only suggesting a way in which such a complex *may* – by chance or by the intuitive skills of performers to a greater or lesser degree improvising – correspond to a complex within a listener's emotional experience and so seem to him valid and perhaps satisfying.

---

[1] See *The Secret Power of Music* by David Taine (Turnstone Press–Thorsons Publishing Group, 1984) from which such gems as the following may be quarried: 'Western string instruments, such as the violin or the guitar have frets upon which an entire melody can be played – even upon a single string.' (p.45); '. . . there are twelve notes to the modern chromatic scale, of which seven are major and five minor'. (p.47).

[2] Frank Muir, *An Irreverent and Thoroughly Incomplete Social History of Almost Everything*, Stein and Day, New York, 1976.

[3] Page 270 et seq.

[4] It could be instructive to carry out an Aaron Copland type exercise (see page 13 ante) to distinguish the nature of despair evoked by the music respectively of Tchaikovsky and Schoenberg.

[5] op.cit. pages 19–20.

[6] Sleeve-note by Per Skans (English translation by John Skinner) to *Six Songs of Experience*, 1970.

[7] Revised edition, 1978.

12
THE PROMOTION OF NEW MUSIC

New Music is a subject in its own right, sustained and advanced by a society devoted to its purpose to whose service I am delighted to have been called by circumstance. With those composers who have contributed their expertise to the practical policy-making of the society and its administration I have shared and contributed to their deliberations the ruminations of an outsider. There may be some advantage in detachment from the energy- and time-consuming problem, for any unknown composer, of how to develop a talent to create new music and also earn a living.

As I have previously remarked, in some other creative fields, notably poetry and painting, public exposure is relatively easy to achieve. Of course the poetry of shy and of rotten poets may never be published. For the shy, this may not matter though for their potential public it may be regrettable: for any writer of doggerel it is only disappointing and the poetaster is lucky to be protected from exposure to a discerning public.

In the case of painting and other visual arts and crafts an opportunity to learn and to practise at school is not uncommon in the United Kingdom; it is open to hardly any would-be composer. A sensitive child may, through experience in school days, acquire either an unhealthy respect or an unwarranted contempt for the work of professional artists. There are artists in the abstract as well as in the

141

representational fields who may teach but still aim to maintain themselves and enhance prestige for eventual commercial advantage primarily by the sale of their works; they should portray a technical ability distinguishing them clearly from the untutored. Successful artists should – but unfortunately cannot always nowadays – be able to depend for their launching more upon *critical* patronage than upon the nose for a promising investment of a patron whose discrimination as a stimulus to his personal generosity is venal rather than cultural; gimmicks, old-boy connections and good fortune winnow out the fashionable from the worthy. As an amateur with no special pretensions other than vanity, I say good luck to them: may patrons, whatever their motives, derive much pleasure from owning their works and, more to the point, hanging them where they will be seen to best advantage – no artist deserves less.

The contemporary composer of music faces virtually no competition from comparison with the work of 'amateurs' (the use of this expression is not to be confused in art with its specialized and abused meanings in relation to sport). Without a grounding in musical theory and a knowledge derived from conscientious practice of at least one musical instrument, there is little likelihood these days of anyone composing any musical work that is not so simple as to sound banal. Contemporary works have to compete with the plethora of music of all ages and kinds performed, recorded, broadcast and heard, even if not listened to, day and night by millions who suppose that they know what they like to hear. The prospects for the amateur in art, literature and, where there is barely a 'professional', poetry, are incomparably better. In music there are few names from former times to recall as specially talented amateurs – Gesualdo, Frederick the Great, Berlioz, Mussorgsky, Rimsky-Korsakov, Borodin, Charles Ives and Lord Berners.

But the lack of unskilled or untaught competition is, sadly, of no avail for the 'young' composer whatever his age. The products of his creative talents, if they are to sound as meaningful as their composer will have intended them to be, must be well-perfomed and exposed to the critical or at least attentive ears of a public. Unless the composer can perform his work by himself alone, having written it for a solo instrument which he has sufficiently mastered, or has at hand generous friends with sufficient skill and time to practise and perform his new work so that he may hear it and decide whether to seek a wider audience, his composition will remain a conglomeration of symbols on paper – indefinitely. That can be frighteningly frustrating to anyone with a creative urge. The risk is that the creative urge will dry up because of the initial non-performance of what has been so laboriously imagined, worked over and written out.

Without highly professional score-reading skills, music must be heard, hence the aim of the SPNM to give aspiring-beginner composers an opportunity to hear their works well performed. If inadequacies of such compositions, perhaps fairly described as student studies, will then be obvious even to the composer that alone will justify the exercise; some lessons simply cannot be learnt in any other way.

It may satisfy some avant-garde artists to create self-destructive works whose effect when they are first perceived is to be instantaneously complete and never to be repeated. Except where the point is the originality of improvisation, that is as clever as a conjuring trick, which may of course be very clever but tends to lack artistic significance. We need not spell out degrees of uniqueness to understand the point. Every time we look at a particular painting the experience is unique – next time, though we are unlikely to realize it, the light will be different, the colours will have faded a little, our vision will have deteriorated slightly too and the 'total environment' of our mood will inevitably have altered. Where pictures can be looked at again and again, the renewed experience will be modified by other intervening experiences which affect the filter of conditioning through which we 'think-see' what we perceive.

No composer, any more than any artist, creates a new work completely outside an historic context. It is pleasant, no doubt, to be able to theorize about a concept of absolute originality; but in our bones we know that it is literally incredible – we could believe it only if we experienced it. This is only one, but an important reason why, in an historical context, it would be exceptional for a creative person working in any medium, not to want others to have an opportunity to appreciate at its best the product of his creativity. Even the most private poems are written down in case their very privacy may some day be shared – or at least chewed over like the cud by the poet later in life, possibly past the last stage of poetic development and in a phase of obsessional narcissism. It would be a mistake to attribute to vanity the almost universal desire to share with others any fruit of creativity.

Ecclesiastes, known as the Preacher, repeatedly condemned 'all' as vanity (I.2 and 14; II.11 and 17 et seq; and XII.8). In the context he was clearly referring to the taking of credit to oneself for doing things and possessing things and wielding power; and to the failure to recognize the impermanence of everything. 'That which hath been is that which shall be; and that which hath been done is that which shall be done: and there is no new thing under the sun' (I.9). He is concerned, as Dr Maurice Nicoll emphasized in his Psychological Commentaries[1] to convey (III.1–8) a sense of the unity of opposites, of the need to transcend them, as in the *Hymn of Jesus*, set to music with the understanding of a mystic, by Gustav Holst.

The urge to share products of creative activity seems at least in part instinctive, as if it were an element in the pre-birth patterning responsible for such human faculties as speech and conceptual thinking. Only by yielding to such an urge can there be realized at one time or another 'that which hath been' and 'that which shall be'; 'that which hath been done' and 'that which shall be done'. We participate willy-nilly in the historical stream of mankind; we draw sustenance from the contributions of others who have preceded us and it may be, through some such process as precognition, from those of our successors too. It seems that anyone who exercises a creative faculty is impelled by the very nature of the stream itself to make his own contribution part of that stream, to help to sustain others and to maintain the continuity of the stream itself. It is a matter of process rather than progress.

The new, the experimental, often seems 'ugly' to its creator's contemporaries; when it is no longer literally new, when it no longer seems experimental it *may* be recognized as 'beautiful' or praised for other admired qualities not generally perceived in it when it was first seen or heard. Examples abound but it will suffice to mention here but two in the realm of music – Beethoven's late quartets; and Stravinsky's *Rite of Spring*. Of course this is to recall the subjectivity of *some* artistic judgements. Currently similar first judgements are referred to electronic music: we are puzzled and perplexed by its never-before-heard sounds and combinations of sounds. We may find them unnatural, at least in music. But then a horn with valves is not 'natural', nor, if it comes to that, is a 'horn' made of brass instead of an animal's horn. There is no special merit in sounds more, rather than less directly derived from a 'natural' source. The human voice is the most natural instrument available to man for music-making yet its use in opera is far from 'natural'.

Curiously, we may find it impossible to listen objectively to an electronic work, or even such a composition written for conventional forces as Brian Ferneyhough's sonatas for string quartet. Do we know what effort is needed to listen 'objectively' to any piece of music, to look at any picture? The effort to do so and therefore the consequential experience are rare because in our culture the left hemisphere of the brain is dominant. By an effort of will, generally neglected but requiring some inner preparation rather than any great expenditure of energy, one may look at pictures with an appreciable degree of objectivity and – why not? – listen similarly to any musical work. I find it almost impossible to look at the great Rembrandt's self-portraits *subjectively*, a degree of objectivity induced in me by that artist's own objectivity. It is as if each of them compels me to look at it with the attributes of the right side of the brain, for its own individual qualities, detached from conditioning or analysis. And then, shortly afterwards, I may find myself – from the left side of the brain again – making comparisons, first with other self-portraits of Rembrandt or with his other portraits and then with self-portraits and portraits painted by other artists.

With music for the non-professional, usually untrained, unpractised music-lover the effort is seldom made to give attention throughout to a work as long as one of Webern's 'miniatures', lasing only seconds or a very few minutes. If made, such an effort is seldom successful – in my case, and I suspect for *most* other people. Though the wandering of the mind and day-dreaming is so familiar to the 'amateur' listener, the varied textures, rhythms and use of tonalities, the logical development and contrast of movements may constantly recall the attention as a piece proceeds. In the world of pop the brevity of each number, each track of an album, more often than not in many radio programmes deliberately curtailed for the next one or some chat or an advert, is effective to maintain the listener's interest. There is an added advantage in that since such music is not considered 'serious' (though it may be much admired) it can be suitably accompanied, without guilty feelings, by idle banter if it is not far too loud, or by suitable matey or mating gestures, set off by each successive change of sound pattern. The insignificance of most of the music, in historical terms, and of the disc-jockey's spiel, except to provide a receptive ear, almost sub-liminally, for the advertisements, is itself insignificant but *more* significant in a wider socio-psychological context.

145

It is doubtful whether more significance can be claimed for serious music, uninterrupted by lazy, habitual, uncontrolled patterns of the mind. This realization, which may enable a kinship to be seen between listening to different kinds of music, may be uncomfortable but nonetheless healthy for a sense of reality. And it may go a little way to explain why many people find contemporary 'serious' music disagreeable. There are fewer opportunities to day-dream in the absence of familiar-sounding or undemandingly repetitive passages. However unattractive we may find the music itself, its unusual qualities constantly attract or re-attract the attention. This can be tiresome and disturbing, and the fact that it makes us more attentive to the music does not compensate for our discomfort. Nor, it seems, does that kind of attentiveness amount to objectivity so as to enable us to judge which of two works has the quality or qualities to justify, to vouchsafe, survival into the era of a future generation of music-lovers who will appreciate it for its true musical worth.

In some cases the problem of assembling an unusual assortment of instruments and sufficiently skilled players militates against frequent performances or even a second performance after a first has been organized under the composer's supervision and perhaps performed by his friends. There may also be problems of notation, not easily overcome, if at all, in the absence of the composer. But – an important innovation – the ability to tape a single performance may provide an opportunity for any interested listener in the future to hear the sounds originally made. If a performance of any work, unique in its generation, is preserved, then in years to come it may be listened to and appreciated, if it so merits, perhaps when the then new music is, in turn, considered too difficult, too unpleasant as sound, to justify even occasional repetition after a first performance.

That prospect is currently rather incestuous. Who will listen to new music *now* except a composer's own contemporaries among composers and a few performers who enjoy the challenge of playing such music? Do performances in these circumstances serve to *promote* new music, and if they do how does this happen? And how else might such music be promoted? These are some of the questions asked frequently amongst SPNM committee members, without the expectation that there are consistent answers which will hold good for very long.

Radio programmes planned without regard for adverse listener ratings must present a special opportunity to promote new music. They can tempt anyone with a musically adventurous spirit and sometimes catch a roving ear linked to knob-twiddling fingers. And the regular notice of references to such a Radio 3 programme as *Music in Our Time* and occasionally the sound of some minutes of it may gradually suggest its normality and imply its acceptability. A consequence of this can be a shift in the subjectivity of casual or deliberate listening from 'How can anyone possibly enjoy this ghastly cacophony?' to 'Well I don't know, but I suppose some people actually like this sort of stuff.' The mind behind the ear is no less conditioned in the latter instance. The complex of perception is still not an 'open ear'. But a tremendous change has occurred, from 'impossible' to 'maybe possible for some, though not for me (– yet)'.

To see the names of contemporary composers on publicity material for concerts is undoubtedly effective in the same way. But it involves the promotion of concerts which are unlikely to prove commercially viable. An empty concert hall is disappointing to the performers and discouraging for the composer. So a contemporary work is, at best, now and again smuggled into a programme of relatively popular music, often relegated to the second half of the programme to give to members of the audience who consider their musical taste barely extends into the twentieth century an excuse to leave at the interval without feeling the need hypocritically to invoke trains to catch or babysitters to relieve. It is uncertain whether this works in the promotion of new music or alternatively puts off a potential audience for both parts of the programme, thus getting the worst of two worlds.

Comparisons between private collections of recorded music can be enlightening about certain facets of the characters of the collectors, where they differ and where they coincide. Charts could be prepared for every collector with attractive coloured shapes filled in to illustrate roughly the scope of their collections – inevitably a *tiny* proportion of the possible. The British Institute of Recorded Sound, founded by Patrick Saul in 1951 to provide for gramophone records an equivalent to the British Library of books at the British Museum, now forms part of that great library as the British Library National Sound Archive and contains currently many more than a quarter of a million micro-groove (LP) records and some 200,000 78s besides, plus cassettes and tapes, of course.

147

But who would have time, never mind inclination, to sample this huge library of recordings with a truly catholic taste? Already the law of diminishing returns oppresses me as my own collection grows and, with days still constricted to twenty-four hours, I recognize that the more records there are the less frequently most of them will be played. And those less often played prove to include a majority of works by relatively unknown composers, which come into the specialist shops unannounced and disappear shortly – sometimes to the bargain racks. A purchase of any of these records is a gamble because there is seldom an opportunity to hear even the opening bars before purchasing. I should therefore explain why, temperamentally, I am prepared to risk disappointment in this way.

When very young I remember my annual support for light blue favours on the day of the Oxford and Cambridge boat race. One year, I think I was six or seven years old, I decided to back Oxford. It cannot have been on a hunch as Cambridge won again – they were on a winning streak in the early 1920s – so I was probably stirred by the wish to console the underdog. When the result of the race was announced, no doubt a foregone conclusion to all the Cambridge supporters around me, the beaming children and their nannies (we had just entered Kensington Gardens from Bayswater Road), I felt an urgent need to hide my inappropriate dark blue rosette and to merge with those other, lucky, ones who had backed the winner. Now I realize, of course, that the underdog is absolutely essential to the principle of a pecking order for dogs. As with those stuck with a 'below-average' label, all struggling to become 'above-average', if there were no underdogs there could be no overdogs. If we don't want clone-dogs, and truly we don't, we must learn to live with a fair ration of underdogs (and they must learn to live with themselves), so as to ensure the survival of highly desirable and much admired overdogs.

Hence I'm in favour of those who, being outsiders, need support if they are not to drop out altogether; whether they also merit support may be less certain. In short, I would wish to encourage the survival and perpetuation of any creative talent, to reduce the risk of merely fashionable popularity (a Top-of-the-Pops syndrome). I am less certain about a curious spin-off from this particular policy – that outsiders might find themselves becoming insiders whether or not they want that; and the change of status and so of outlook would be likely to distort the nature and quality of their creative output. So I incline to a fatalistic attitude regarding the possible results of my musico-social policy.

It follows that my collection of records of contemporary music, most of it music unheard by me until the record has been bought and I play it for the first time, contains a great many flops – academic exercises and student essays, as they seem, whether the composers were in reality young or old when composing them. Were it not for their efforts and my and the recording sponsors' patronage I am convinced that we could never expect to nurture and indeed would never deserve to hear the work of any contemporary musical genius.

Music, as a distinct art-form, is all of a piece from the past into the future, irrespective of the level of brow to which it may appeal. If I were to deny to my children reasonable opportunities to listen to the music they currently enjoy I should not expect to be allowed to listen in peace to 'my' most peculiar kind of music. There is a largely unrecognized cross-fertilization in listening just as there is a recognized one in composition. Benny Goodman on the clarinet, Menuhin with Grappelli, Johnny Dankworth, Gershwin, Copland, Stravinsky, Walton, Constant Lambert, Charles Ives and many others only evidence the tip of the flirtation between jazz and classical music. The influence of folk and dance music on classical forms and melodies, at any time from Bach to Bartok – and they are not at the extremes of course – is extensive and unrestricted as to countries – Beethoven, Mendelssohn, Bloch and others from all over the world of Western music used Scottish themes, for example. These days, one's listening is inevitably catholic, whatever one's taste. Hence what I have called 'cross-fertilization' may often be subliminal for listeners and an openness to new musical experience may happen without need for conscious effort.

What may be seen as essential elements in the 'development' or 'evolution' of musical style and form through the last six hundred years or so of Western music may perhaps be more appropriately recognized as the interconnected constituents of a far from sluggish stream. It is in the light of this vision of continuity that especially idiosyncratic composers or works may be seen, or rather heard, for their exceptional contribution to the most moving, most interesting, most colourful or most significant characteristics of one or another 'incident' in the swirling torrent or in a relatively stagnant backwater.

Edward Greenfield[2] is evidently convinced that 'Constant Lambert's gloomy predictions in *Music Ho!* half a century ago about an art in decline look ever more accurate . . . The avant garde explosion has simply fragmented.' I believe that he has misread the signs – or read only wrong signs, and that in reality nothing short of physical catastrophe on an almost global scale could staunch the flow. No decrees of a philistine autocracy currently terminate the composition and performance of more and more electronic music, including instrumental music with an electronic dimension. If it must be composed some of it will, sooner or later, be heard. Then, if it does not over-strain performing resources and if it sounds attractive enough from any point of view, it will be repeated and may be recorded. There is a kind of socio-moral obligation on 'amateur listeners', falling nevertheless far short of a moral imperative, to spare time and attention generously to listen to the ever-freshly conceived music with a deliberately open ear. We don't have to be masochistic often; or martyrs. Only sometimes, and then not in perpetuity.

---

[1] *Psychological Commentaries on the Teaching of Gurdjieff and Ouspensky*, Vincent Stuart, London, 1952; Vol.I, page 321.
[2] *Guardian* 17 December 1979.

13
THERAPY

Lady Hunstanton: Music makes one feel so romantic – at least it always gets on one's nerves.

Mrs Allonby: I'm so glad I don't know what you mean, dear. I'm afraid you mean something wrong.

A Woman of No Importance, Oscar Wilde.

'What Mrs Allonby means, of course . . . is that music like everything else in her life gets on her nerves.'[1] What Wilde has Lady Hunstanton suspecting is that Mrs Allonby is referring to a feeling of guilt over romantic feelings, reflecting a wish to be involved in some morally naughty situation.

Woody Allen, an incomparably witty and a paradoxically objective commentator on the moods and mores of the modern Manhattan equivalent of the Bloomsbury set and of a segment of our mid-Atlantic society, was quoted in the *Observer* some years ago as replying to the question 'Is sex dirty?' – 'Only if it's done right.' One sees, on reflection at least, what he means; his comment is at once more exact and more subtle than D. H. Lawrence's on pornography as 'doing dirt on sex'.

A concept that there is a right way to make music would be equally misguided. Yet in reviewing concerts, or performances on record, critics who are free to make comparisons with other performances often choose to write as if there were just one right way to perform a particular phrase, a movement or the whole work. Sometimes a performance ideally conducted by or based on rehearsals effectively 'supervised' by the composer – if there were only one such performance and that known to and memorized by the critic – may seem to give warranty for his puristic opinion. But any serious critic will know that the concept of such purity is nonsense; his own fallible, conditioned, subjective judgement on the occasion when he heard the performance he is reviewing *or* when he came to write the review is, in reality, the only applicable basis for his pontification – never mind that a composer may not know how to perform his work, may even underestimate its potential in terms of musical sense, coherence or sound.

I have written of music's function to remind one of the moods and emotions experienced at other times, perhaps below the threshold of consciousness. Its function is also to refresh the mind, in all *its* functions. If it were assumed that a popular tune, say *Roses of Picardy*, played by the mechanism of a musical box, were thereby definitively performed, it would be wrong or silly to listen to it if it were performed otherwise: then it would be *pointless* to wind up and play it on the musical box. Any mechanically or electrically repeatable performance is recognized as a substitute only for a live performance. This may seem to apply to the actual live performance recorded but in reality it is true for every other possible live performance. Indeed there is a sense in which each live performance is a substitute for every other!

If my surmise is valid it may be assumed that a work 'composed' by a computer and performed electronically can give a feeling of satisfaction only if the same work might also be presented in a quite different way. I am virtually postulating as an additional definition of music, 'a sequence and combination of sounds audible to human beings which may be heard more than once recognizably, though possibly modified in performance, no matter how'.

This factor of being-capable-of-being-differently-performed, so that there is no question of a performance being valid 'only if it's done right', is, though significant, perhaps tangential to my concern to observe the effect of listening to music while performing various physical and mental tasks. Nevertheless where my emotions in creative activities, such as painting and writing poetry, are involved or where I am inclined to listen with special attention otherwise than at a concert, for instance at a memorial service for someone for whom I greatly grieve and any other solemn occasion, there seems to be a need for an 'openness' about the music itself which could not be projected in a once-and-for-always absolutely mechanical piece.

One effect of music on me is to break up tensions in the thought and feeling processes. It might concentrate and magnify such tensions for others. How it effects a relaxation of tensions I do not know nor do I have the facilities or skills necessary to determine, if this were possible, how to find out. The more 'mechanical' the music perceived, negating the freedom or implied freedom to vary it, the less effective it is for the purpose for which I believe most music is, these days, listened to or tolerated. In a negative sense my belief is reinforced by the powerful antipathy I feel for any music which fails to induce in me any expectation of the possibility of a variation from the obvious. Much pop music (though, recordings apart, performances will usually differ widely) has me distracted and agitated by its coincidental rhythmic insistence and, as it seems to me, underlying triviality. I find my reactions are much the same to light music – it is a ghastly torment. In either variety of music a variation in the manner or effect of performance – possible, of *course* – would not in the slightest degree reduce my acute agitation and fury at the unwelcome distraction which such (to me) hideously boring music exclusively provides.

So, a partial and partly subliminal distraction – on my terms – I find agreeable and I believe therapeutic. Complete distraction by music that I happen to find uninteresting if not positively disagreeable, raises my blood-pressure, increasing rather than resolving tensions, and has, I am sure, other harmful effects too obscure to be listed.

The effect of the *valuable* influence of music seems to be a relaxation of subconscious tensions which inhibit the fruitful functioning of those parts of the mind engaged on the task in question. It is as if spontaneous inflections in the way the music is performed suggest to hidden parts of the mind significant but perhaps barely perceptible inflections in my performance of the task in hand. I regard this as more direct than a reminder: it is more like the inducement of a correspondence, as of resonance between two violin strings tuned to the same pitch – the vibration of one inducing a like vibration in the other; or the passage of electric current into a wire lying close to another charged with a current from some power source. The effect I have described as similar to a transference of an electrical force might as tellingly be compared to the loosening of rubbish at the grating to a drain, enabling water to pass through.

Any of the music I listen to for the purpose I have just described might well produce for others an effect such as pop or light music provide for me; it may have no perceptible beneficial effect. But perhaps those who enjoy and choose to listen to music with more or less attention when they are *not* engaged in doing anything in particular may benefit, just as I claim to benefit by listening while I am working – certain rigidities in the mind are relaxed or dissolved, so that finer energies may filter in and circulate.[2]

'All music improvisations are to some extent premeditated,' wrote a music critic, Meirion Bowen,[3] close to a suggestion which I have already made. But it is important to qualify the apparent absoluteness of this generalization. There is one form of musical improvisation which has long intrigued me and which it would seem could be in no sense premeditated – the music improvised by the wind on an aeolian harp.

Aeolus, the god and ruler of winds, was the son of Hippotus and of Menecla the daughter of Hyllus, King of Lipara. He dwelt (according to William King[4]) in the island of Strongyle, like Lipara one of the seven Aeolian islands; or else at Rhegium in Italy.

Now a modern protagonist of the aeolian harp, Robert Archer, has produced a record of aeolian harp music played by the summer winds of the British Isles unaided, as he says, by mortal's touch, on the Tor at Glastonbury, the Malvern Hills, Iona in the Hebrides, by Derwent Water in the Lake District and elsewhere. He tells of the ancient Greek legend that 'when Orpheus was murdered by Thracian Bacchanals his harp was thrown into the River Hebrus with his severed head upon it. The harp, touched by the wind, breathed forth a solemn strain. Later, this lyre was suspended in the temple of Apollo' where its sounds may have been 'reserved for initiates of the Mysteries'; and perhaps, too, served to silence with awe the uninitiated.

Archer suggests that in more recent times Athanasius Kircher, a Jesuit priest at Rome, probably designed and made the first instrument intended to play in the wind, in the mid-seventeenth century. Looking to the possibility of development in the future, Archer mentions his 'fantasy about one day building a huge aeolian harp in a specially

154

constructed temple set on a mountainside. There would be coloured lights and perfumes to accompany the music.' 'Scent et lumière' nearly sets me against encouraging any development at all; but not quite. There *is* something, I believe, in Archer's line of speculation: 'In this "scientific" and mechanistic age, physical phenomena are generally ascribed to physical causes. Thus the harp's music may be attributed solely to the air-flow over the strings. Personally, I consider this a narrow, limited view, which confuses effects and causes. Fortunately, poets and artists have long balanced this soul-less, "scientific" attitude, with their intuitions about existence.'

He then describes aeolian harp music, composed and played by the wind without any human assistance as 'probably the ultimate in natural music. It is this unique method of string activation which creates the totally non-percussive tones, and the complex melodies, harmonies, crescendos and diminuendos of the music. This can provide a balm which soothes the psyche; an antidote for the strident and percussive sounds of the machinery and even the avant-garde "music" of this age.' He continues: 'The harp music has a number of interesting effects. It stills the wind – useful for those who wish to meditate or simply to rest and relax. It also seems to train the ear to perceive harmony in place of noise. Immediately after listening to the harp, on two occasions, I have for an instant heard the most magnificent symphony created by the wind in trees, and by waves. The sound of the harp may just be a small step on the way to our perception of the hidden music and meaning in all natural sounds, many of which we do not comprehend and dismiss as "noise".'

Bela Bartok, even in his last, miserable years in America – miserable because of a shortage of money, the burden and pain of the illness, leukemia (and the X-ray treatment for it), from which he suffered and eventually died in New York on 26 September 1945 and, underlying these circumstances, the tragic news which reached him from his beloved Hungary, ravaged by war – retained an exceptional sensitivity to natural sounds and other natural emanations, as Agatha Fassett, a biographer of his last years in America, tells.[5] She quotes his wife, Ditta, as saying – when Bartok suddenly announced in the middle of Sixty-sixth Street, New York, 'I smell horses' – 'Bela is always smelling and hearing things no one else can smell or hear. The strange thing is that no matter how wrong he seems, he's always right.' And so he was on that occasion, when he crossed the street and stood in the entrance to the stable of a riding academy.

It must be acknowledged that Bartok listening to music and sensing natural emanations, seems not always, as in the case of the smell of horses in the middle of New York, to have experienced the balm which Robert Archer attributes to music of the aeolian harp and which I attribute to whatever music seems to suit any particular individual at any particular time for comfort or reassurance.

Gladly provoked into communicating with Archer by an illustrated talk he gave on Radio 3 which I chanced to hear in the autumn of 1979, I was struck by a reference to Berlioz' *Lelio*, called 'the craziest work ever sketched out by a composer not actually insane'.[6] In that hotchpotch of a composition an interlude called 'The Aeolian Harp' is 'an impressionist reminiscence' of a Song of Bliss derived from Berlioz' *Orpheus* cantata. Unfortunately Berlioz' intended effect doesn't *quite* hum; I wish he could try again.

Elgar was a composer known to have appreciated the sound of the aeolian harp. After Archer's talk, I wondered whether Elgar might ever have introduced into the music he composed some more successful representation of that strange sound. Almost at once I realized where he had done just that – in the most magical passage of all his music, the curiously evocative cadenza for the solo instrument, accompanied by tremolo strings, in the last movement of his violin concerto. Evocative of what else than the aeolian harp's realization of the sound of gentle breezes? Donald Tovey, for years the doyen of music critics, wrote of this:

Suddenly the music dies away into the minor, and the themes of the first movement reappear slowly and mysteriously in the cadenza, which has become famous as one of the most original dialogues between a solo instrument and an orchestra that have ever been imagined. The device of the 'pizzicato tremolo', which Elgar has invented in this passage, ought henceforth to be a matter of common knowledge in orchestral music. There is nothing like it for filmy harmonious transparency and mystery; and it is one of the simplest things in the world. But we wrong this cadenza if we ascribe its aesthetic value to an orchestral effect. The priceless thing is to find such devices invented in the service of music which enshrines a soul. It is not a sensational effect; and those who have heard of it by reputation and expect to be startled by it will be disappointed. It is simply a commonsense solution to the problem of providing an exquisitely faint harmony that will keep entirely in the background on any notes required.[7]

This concerto was dedicated by Elgar in Spanish in these words 'Aqui esta encerrada el alma de . . . . . (1910)' – 'Herein is enshrined the soul of . . . . .' Five dots rather than three! Lady Elgar is said to have told Dorabella of the *Enigma* variations (Mrs Richard Powell) that Julia Worthington was the unnamed dedicatee. A closer friend of Elgar's, Alice Stuart-Wortley, has been suggested as a more likely candidate for whom Elgar's nickname was 'Windflower'; Eric Mason says in a sleeve-note to the Zuckerman recording that 'while composing the concerto Elgar wrote to her that he had been "working hard at the wind flower themes – but all stands until you come and approve".' Elgar's own soul? Or, just conceivably that of Aeolus himself?

Then, in early October 1979, I heard Elaine Padmore talking in advance about the music she had selected to present in a Radio 3 *Play It Again* programme. In her 'trail' a short excerpt was broadcast from Paul Rovsing Olsen's *How to play in D major without letting anybody know about it* for two accordions. The full programme of three works for this unusual duo was to be broadcast in mid-afternoon on a subsequent Saturday.

In order not to miss the whole work, whether it occurred nearer to 2.00 p.m. or 5.00 p.m., I rearranged my Saturday afternoon. The Olsen work should have been the first item, at 2.00 p.m. But to my unabated fury, in substitution for *How to play in D major . . .* etc. I heard only a light three-movement work, also for two accordions of course, but of absolutely no interest to me. I protested to the BBC duty officer by telephone at once and at his suggestion then wrote to Clive Bennett whose name was given to me as the 'responsible producer', Music Division, to ask if he would enable me to acquire a tape of the one work which I had wanted to hear or to tape it as permitted by my Amateur Recording Licence. I also wrote, 'If *Play It Again* is to raise and then shatter legitimate expectations I will regard it as contributing disgracefully to a slippery slope of trivialization.'

There followed a brief exchange of letters with Bennett:

Friday 9 November 1979
Dear Mr Rubinstein,
Thank you for your letter of 20 October 1979.

You refer to me as 'the responsible producer'. Surely you meant either 'irresponsible producer' or 'producer responsible'. You also use the phrase 'fobbed off', the emotional character of which begs all manner of questions. You misspell 'excerpt' each time you use it. You mix metaphors to odd effect.

I am afraid I have spent far too many evenings among your legal colleagues to overlook this untidy use of English. You will understand why the revelation of your profession cuts little ice in this office.

But to be serious, I am sorry you misunderstood Elaine Padmore's trails. What she said was that this was the *kind* of sound you could hear on the programme, not this was the *piece* you could hear. Now you might argue that by that token we could trail Bruckner's Ninth with Bruckner's Seventh and so we could. The sonic aspect is very similar, the emotional one quite dissimilar. With the novel noise of two accordions the surface timbre is fascinating, so to try to capture our listeners' attentions we chose something unlike any other music – the weird phasing effect of *How to play in D* . . . But for the programme we wanted a different *emotional* effect; hence the choice of Lundquist's *Ballad*. At no point did we claim we were going to play *How to play in D* . . .

There is no possibility of us providing you with a copy of the work; to do so would be to infringe all the copyrights you so carefully accept in your recording ventures. All I can offer is the possibility of the entire programme being repeated some time in the future.

I assume the last paragraph of your letter – about legitimate expectations and the slippery slopes of trivialization – to be as deliberately provocative and facetious as my opening one, and therefore that it requires no further comment.

Yours sincerely,
Clive Bennett

13 November 1979
Dear Mr Bennett,

Thank you for your letter of the 9 November, validly criticizing me for misspelling a word more than once, untidy use of English, stylistic errors and using a phrase whose emotional character begged 'all manner of questions' (cliché?). *Mea culpa*. I hope that makes you happy.

So I 'misunderstood Elaine Padmore's trails', my fault for distinguishing between 'the *kind* of sound' I expected to hear on the *Play It Again* programme and the *piece* I actually heard. Never mind that I might argue this or that about two Bruckner symphonies, one the *kind* of sound you could use to trail the other *piece*. I don't happen to like Bruckner.

You didn't know and, I am astonished to learn from your letter, do not appear to care that one listener at least – he happened to be me – was interested in precisely the *kind* of sound made by the two accordions in *How to play in D . . . .* But for the programme you wanted a different *emotional* effect. You say yourself that you tried to capture your listeners' attentions by choosing 'something unlike any other music – the weird phasing effect of *How to play in D . . .*'. Why did it not then or, later, when you came to reply to my letter strike you that to capture the attention of any of your listeners with an unusual *kind* of sound entitled such a listener to expect to hear the piece which uniquely *conveyed* that kind of sound and not a different piece (which happened to be for the same instrumental combination) which you chose because *you* wanted 'a different *emotional* effect'. That is 'fobbing off' – the phrase is exactly right. I didn't *misunderstand* Elaine Padmore's trail: the trail *misled* me. *Tua culpa* – and don't expect me to apologize for untidy Latin.

Alas the last paragraph of my letter was not 'deliberately provocative and facetious': it was deliberately provocative and absolutely serious.

As I mentioned in my previous letter I am writing a book about the way non-professional music-lovers listen to music. I was trying to trace works with a *particular* weird sound effect. *How to play in D . . .* heard fleetingly in the trailer was only the third piece I had traced producing this curious effect. I do not doubt your assurance that Elaine Padmore said that 'this was the *kind* of sound' listeners could hear on the programme. I claim that my expectation that I would hear *that* kind of sound was legitimate. Not only was another piece substituted for *How to play in D . . .* but it was *not* 'the *kind* of sound' I was expecting: of course it wasn't – you had deliberately chosen 'something unlike any other music' to capture my attention, when 'for the programme [you] wanted a different *emotional* effect'. You got one! I was very angry indeed: legitimately.

It is a matter for you to consider whether, your assumption about the last paragraph of my letter being, as I have explained, mistaken, you will now after all comment further. You have reinforced my serious concern that the use of the 'trail' on this occasion was an example of trivialization – like a picture of a bikini-clad model on a beach to advertise a seaside holiday: I may be a gullible sexist male but I know I can't expect to meet *her* when I take my family to the advertised resort. Do you see what I'm getting at?

Can you begin to understand my frustration, my feeling of outrage, when you write 'All I can offer is the *possibility* of the entire programme being repeated *some time in the future*' (my emphasis)? To provide me with a copy of the work 'would be to infringe all the copyrights you so carefully accept in your recording ventures', you say. What, in Heaven's name, are you on about – all the copyrights I so carefully accept in my recording ventures? To publish this pathetic exchange of correspondence in my book will be no consolation for the lost opportunity to hear *How to play in D* . . . . And you have the petty-mindedness to rabbit on about infringement of copyright! First you fob off and now you rabbit on. God save Radio 3! If it isn't too late.

Yours sincerely,
Michael Rubinstein

Friday 16 November 1979
Dear Mr Rubinstein,

Thank you for your second letter.

We must agree to differ over our interpretation of the intention, comprehensibility and triviality content of Elaine Padmore's trail of *Play It Again.* I accept that for you the sound of *How to play in D* . . . was of greater interest than any intrinsic musical value the piece may, or may not, have contained. Ms Padmore and I believed that its opening bars were more extraodinary [*sic*] and more arresting than the remainder of its musical content; but of course this you will be able to evaluate when, or rather if Radio 3 repeat it. That you felt you were misled into expecting the sound unique to that piece rather than a variety of sounds unique to that combination of instruments was unfortunate, even regrettable. I do hope that the anger it provoked has not had a lasting effect.

I am afraid I must take issue with you on the copyright position. To point out why the BBC will not make the illegal copy you (or anyone else) request is a demonstration not of 'petty-mindedness' rabbitting on but of safeguarding legitimate interests against potential predators.

By the way, you choose the words 'fob off' and 'rabbit on' to describe my actions. Insults do not clarify the mind or induce sympathetic consideration of argument. Let us get mole-hills into perspective; it reveals the mountains as more significant.

Yours sincerely,
Clive Bennett

While this pathetic correspondence was being exchanged – with its crude brush-off suggesting that the BBC was right to refuse a request I had not made that it should provide me with an illegal copy of its tape not elsewhere obtainable – I was involved in a controversy with the British Phonographic Industry, over the relevant but incomprehensible provisions of the Copyright Act 1956 and of the Licence itself, in a series of monthly issues of the Law Society's *Guardian Gazette* read by hardly anyone who is not a lawyer. For composers, performers and manufacturers of recordings, I would wish to uphold the justice of copyright restrictions on taping music, especially from commercial records and from the radio. But I deplore the industry's efforts to seek, through secret lobbying and piecemeal legislation, inequitable and unenforceable redress against domestic and commercial pirating of legally protected material. I had widely publicized statistics that, to be kind, I found utterly unconvincing to justify its oppressive proposals. Whether or not the widespread use of recording equipment, much of it produced, together with blank cassettes, by the very record manufacturers who were complaining of it, was in fact responsible for the industry's alleged near ruin I have reason to doubt; their proffered statistics were to my untutored mind meaningless rather than inconclusive. But the industry itself acknowledged that the pop music fans who borrowed records to tape would, if reprimanded, tell the industry 'to get stuffed'. And its new proposals would, it seemed to me, invite even coarser evidence of contempt for the law in realms where offenders against it could not, in practice, be detected.

Significant though the details of this digression may be in relation to the commercial exploitation of a hunger, rather than a taste, for short musical pieces very loudly amplified, largely created by the industry's own market miscalculations and false, eternal-growth orientated

161

economic philosophy, my concern here is with sound effects and not with sound policies. So – on to my fourth, and perhaps most dubious, example of a classical/modern work which might well have been inspired by the aeolian harp.

This is the first sonata in F minor, Op.80, for violin and piano, written between 1938 and 1946, by Prokofiev (whom I regard, incidentally, as the harmonic heir to Richard Strauss). Anyone who appreciates the monumental in a sonata and yet does not know this work should hasten to hear it. Joseph Szigeti once wrote of it, 'What Prokofiev, with the reticence typical of him, did not say is that the whole work seems conceived on a scale of Moussorgsky, an epic grandeur . . .'[8] But Prokofiev *did* apparently comment to Oistrakh père who inspired it, that the wild but quiet runs up and down a strange scale by the violin, against gently played chords on the piano, were 'like the wind in a graveyard'.[9] The description is close enough to satisfy me that if Prokofiev had never heard an aeolian harp when he wrote that movement he had acquired an exceptional aural imagination in a real graveyard somewhere.

Probably in the course of time I shall discover further examples of composed music intentionally or incidentally resembling the sound of an aeolian harp. It may not be found where it could be expected. Chopin provides wild arpeggios up and down the piano, for instance in the last movement of his piano sonata in B flat minor, just as Prokofiev has the violin rushing up and down in that sonata. It may be that the harmonic bases of Chopin's arpeggios rule them out as simulating the wind in the harp's strings even in his *Étude* Op.25 No.1, nicknamed – in the USA! – 'The Aeolian Harp', it is said on account of Chopin's performance as described by Schumann. Chopin might indeed have been expected to have heard the instrument and could well have been attracted by the romantic element, if not by the mystical.

Debussy will of course have heard the sound of wild winds before he wrote his three symphonic sketches, *La Mer*, with a movement entitled 'Dialogue of the Wind and of the Sea'. But here, too, composed music inbred with the magic of genius depicts the raw subject in magnificent impressionistic gestures probably uninfluenced by the natural harmonics of the aeolian harp, mysterious only to our conditioned ears. Electronic music and electronically 'enhanced' music may be devised or more likely may chance to sound like the aeolian harp – *Pashanti* by David Evan Jones is an example in which harp-like chords are built up by wind instruments. Listen, however, to the start of the tenebroso section of the fifth, scherzo movement of Alban Berg's lyric suite for string quartet . . . Or to the first five minutes or so of Nigel Osborne's *Mythologies*.

In a moment of inspiration, I pursued this peculiar line of research by referring my interest to the British Institute of Recorded Sound, as it then was. There I found myself listening to a record of Henry Cowell, an experimental American composer, friend of Charles Ives, playing one of his own piano compositions – *Aeolian Harp* (1923) – and playing it, as scored, partly inside the piano. Perhaps not surprisingly the piece sounded more like that than like an aeolian harp; but it was a worthy essay just the same.

And on the same occasion I was delighted to listen to a tape of that very BBC Radio 3 broadcast of *How to play in D major without letting anybody know about it* by Paul Rovsing Olsen which Clive Bennett, the producer responsible, had so harshly denied me. What a pity that he had not told me of this admirable facility, provided by the Sound Archive in co-operation with the Corporation; but then (silver cloud) we would never have indulged in that colourful correspondence . . .

Had I heard of Hugo Wolf's song to a poem of Mörike *To the Aeolian Harp*? Or of Sergius Mikhailovich Liapounov's study for piano (no doubt one of twelve *Études d'execution transcendante*) Op.11 No.9? Eric Hughes of the Sound Archive plucked these nuggets of information, sleepless at night when he must have searched the wind to help me, from his exceptional knowledge. Taking advantage of his powers of recall to listen to those pieces, made available to me through the Archive's facilities for researchers, I have to report first that neither it nor I can trace any currently available recording of Schumann's setting of the Mörike poem. Wolf's, not surprisingly, is a beautiful song and I find it in keeping with the poet's inspiration – the death of a young brother. Joan Chissell, in a sleeve-note to an excellent recording of Elizabeth Schwartzkopf accompanied by Geoffrey Parsons, writes that Hugo Wolf 'never having heard an aeolian harp when writing this extended, freely unfolding song . . . was delighted to come upon one in an old castle seven weeks later and discover how exactly it corresponded to his imaginings'. But not, alas, to mine!

The Brahms setting of the same poem, Op.95 No.5 has been more frequently recorded, it seems. At the Institute (as it then was) I heard Helen Watts accompanied by Irwin Gage and I bought records of Elsa

Cavelti (with Geoffrey Parsons), in 1972 obviously long past her prime, and Norma Procter (with Paul Hamburger) making lovely Brahmsian sounds but still less like those of an aeolian harp than Wolf's setting, if that were possible.

And then, on a record with Berg's *Sieben frühe Lieder* (1907), I discovered music much closer to the authentic sound of strings inspired by the wind, in a work recorded in 1976 by the soprano Taru Valjakka with the Austrian Radio Symphony Orchestra conducted by the composer Leif Segerstam. I commend Segerstam as a twentieth-century composer who will eventually be appreciated like Robert Simpson for his string quartets if for nothing else – though he is also a talented violinist and pianist as well as conductor. In his *Six Songs of Experience* (1971) set to four poems by Blake and two by Auden, Segerstam sustains the magical 'feel' of the aeolian harp as well as a sense of its actual sounds, notably in 'The Fly' (Blake), and in 'Orpheus' (Auden).

The object of art may be to improve on nature, but artifacts such as the aeolian harp may enable nature to improve on itself. In the early years of this century Groves (1904 edition) reported that the Chinese had kites with vibrating strings and the Malays had 'a curious aeolian instrument, a rough bamboo cane of considerable height, perforated with holes and stuck in the ground'. Earlier, 'according to tradition King David's harp (*kinnor*) sounded at midnight when suspended over his couch in the north wind; and in an old Hindu poem, quoted by Sir William Jones, the *vina*, or lute of the country, is said to have produced tones, proceeding by musical intervals, by the impulse of the breeze'. And in the tenth century 'St Dunstan of Canterbury is said to have hung his harp so that the wind might pass between the strings and to have been accused of sorcery in consequence'. Now Max Eastley has developed a range of Sound Sculptures which enable unpredictable music to emerge from the force of flowing water, vibrating strings much as the wind may do; rotating strips of bamboo may be played by a tumbling wooden ball like a randomly struck xylophone; and strips of latex can sing in the wind, like birds – even imitated by starlings in their audience.

If I am an expert amateur listener to a relatively restricted range of music, I am a relative ignoramus on the subject of music used therapeutically. Its use has been increasingly promoted in this country, largely through the active propagation and work of the British Society for Music Therapy under the guidance of its late founder and chairman, Juliette Alvin. In an article entitled 'A humanistic approach to music therapy'[10] she referred to two main paths to music therapy techniques, the active and the receptive. She added:

> Therapeutic approaches should help man to become conscious of the way he uses music as a means of communication, and what he reveals in the process. Free musical improvisation is one of the most effective techniques through which the patient expresses spontaneously and sometimes unconsciously what he feels, on an instrument requiring no musical education or techniques. This approach eliminates the conditioning acquired in learning music. It by-passes intellectual, inhibiting processes and can release emotional material buried in the subconscious. The value of such release cannot be underestimated [*sic*] provided that it is done under proper psychological control. Then the most intimate communication can be established between the inner life of the patient and his consciousness.

Without decrying its benefit to patients who have participated in music therapy, there is, for those not afflicted at least, another twist to an approach which 'eliminates the conditioning acquired in learning music'. It by-passes also the psychic and physical rewards of doing the work and learning the discipline and technique.

The value of therapeutic methods, using music and its rhythms to inspire movement and corresponding emotional stirrings and releases, is undoubted among all those who have studied and experienced their practice. The twentieth-century pioneer in this field, though he taught primarily those not in obvious need of therapy, was Emile Jaques-Dalcroze. As he put it '. . . musical sensations of a rhythmic nature call for the muscular and nervous response of the *whole organism*. I set my pupils exercises in stepping and halting, and trained them to react physically to the perception of musical rhythms. That was the origin of my "Eurhythmic" . . .'(his emphasis).[11]

Dalcroze devised his exercises to enable those participating 'to utilize their powers, to attain due balance, and thereby to adapt themselves to the necessities of their individual and collective existence'.

He aimed to train children, especially, by his system – but the training is surely no less apt for adults – 'to become conscious of their personalities, to develop their temperaments, and to liberate their particular rhythms of individual life from every trammelling influence. More than ever they should be enlightened as to the relations existing between soul and mind, between the conscious and the subconscious, between imagination and the processes of action. Thoughts should be brought into immediate contact with behaviour – the new education aiming at regulating the interaction between our nervous and our intellectual forces. Fresh from the trenches, soldiers should be able to continue the struggle in a new guise; and in the schools our teachers, likewise, should be on the alert to combat weakness of will and lack of confidence, and to train the fresh generations by every possible means to fight for self-mastery and the power to place themselves, fully equipped, at the service of the human race.'[12]

It requires no cynicism, only a touch of realism, to recognize in these high-flown over-optimistic phrases an idealist's recipe for failure or at least for non-success. Dalcroze did devise a system for teaching children to listen and move with attention, with an unusual degree of co-ordination and with the freedom derived from the practice of harmonized control. But a dimension was missing, or perhaps more than one. Later, in 1922, Gurdjieff taught a psychological and cosmological system, largely Sufi in origin, at the Institute for the Harmonious Development of Man which he established in the Prieuré, in Avon near Fontainebleau. The institute was not orientated to accommodate the soldiers 'fresh from the trenches . . . to continue the struggle in a new guise' but offered to men and women a way to realize their innate potentials through exceptional individual and group effort.

Since his system was designed expressly to avoid exaggerated expressions of faculties or functions in thought or emotion, there was equal concern to develop the co-ordination of physical manifestations in harmony with the others. Thus Gurdjieff built on Dalcroze's foundations. The 'movements' he devised, exercises and dances, were to be practised and performed, with exceptional attention, to music composed specially, in many instances by Thomas de Hartman under Gurdjieff's guidance. It was unsentimental even when sinuous and flowing. If it had been primarily beautiful, striking or exciting music it would obviously have been useless for his purpose: it would have attracted undue emotional attention and so thrown out of balance the essential overall scheme. 'Beauty does not lead to God, beauty only leads us to beauty.'[13]

Art-forms are not the conveyors of beauty only; they cannot exclude ugliness. These subjectively recognized opposites and a third alternative, tedium, constitute the 'package' to attract, repel or distract, much as do camouflage and superficial sense-perceived characteristics in the animal kingdom. We may be hypnotized by the form and so miss that which is packaged, the content, i.e. the musical features of a particular work to which we are listening; the work conveys messages to us irrespective of whether we like it in whole, in part or not at all. And these messages may be and generally are received quite differently by every listener. Listeners receive the same messages differently because of the varying scope of their listening experiences including the distinct kinds of listening which can be derived only from personal participation in music-making. 'Messages' conveyed by music will be distinct according to the associations – or lack of them – for each listener, drawn to and clustered round every phrase and the whole of every movement and work.

Perhaps the earliest story on record of the therapeutic effect of music is to be found in the Old Testament, in I Samuel. When David first came to Saul and stood before him it is said Saul 'loved him greatly'. David had been commended to Saul as 'a cunning player on the harp' to relieve Saul from his mental distress when he was troubled by 'an evil spirit from God', who had rejected him, through the medium of Samuel, for disobedience. The Israelites' vengeful God ordered Saul to 'go and smite Amalek, and utterly destroy all that they have, and spare them not; but slay both man and woman, infant and suckling, ox and sheep, camel and ass', the Amalekites having incurred His wrath by attacking some Israelite girls in the Wilderness in the course of their forty-year passage from Egypt to Moses' Promised Land. Saul had inexcusably spared Agag, the king of the Amalekites, as well as the best of their cattle, not wholly motivated by mercy it would seem.

Whatever name might nowadays be given to the 'evil spirit', Christopher Fowkes in *A Life of Rembrandt*[14] calls it schizophrenia, a disease of the mind which, he writes, Rembrandt could understand because 'he had recognized in himself the tendency of the human mind to distance itself from a reality which is too painful . . . caused by essentially the same mechanism'. Fowkes was commenting on one of

Rembrandt's most moving paintings, known as 'David harping before Saul', which depicts the last verse in Chapter 16 of I Samuel: 'And it came to pass, when the spirit from God was upon Saul, that David took the harp, and played with his hand: so Saul was refreshed, and was well, and the evil spirit departed from him.'

Fowkes adds: 'Saul, who has outbursts of violence, has David to play the harp for him to soothe the "evil spirit". But God has withdrawn his favour from the king bestowing it instead on David, and in his grief and jealousy Saul will attempt to "smite David even to the wall" with his spear. In a brilliantly intuitive painting Rembrandt has understood the nature of Saul's illness, and shows him in the moment of balance when grief becomes violence – already the muscles of his hand tense ready to grasp the weapon. But the painting contains one final surprise. The curtain which divides David and Saul is an image which has been used by twentieth-century psychologists when attempting to describe the detachment from the environment which occurs in schizophrenia.'

In Chapter 18, however, after the story of David's victory over Goliath, Saul is said for the first time to have cast the spear and attempted 'to smite David even to the wall'. That was on the day after the women had come 'out of all the cities of Israel, singing and dancing to meet king Saul, with timbrels, with joy, and with instruments of music. And the women sang one to another in their play, and said, Saul hath slain his thousands, and David his ten thousands. And Saul was very wroth and this saying displeased him . . .' (He had another cause of intense jealousy of David: Jonathan, Saul's son, 'loved him as his own soul', a love evidently reciprocated.) David, playing the harp for the violently troubled Saul, on this occasion twice avoided being speared to the wall. And David again escaped such a fate (Chapter 19), playing for Saul when 'an evil spirit of the Lord was upon him', after Saul had given him the hand of his daughter Michal for bringing him two hundred foreskins from slaughtered Philistines, when he had sent David to bring him only one hundred instead of a dowry, expecting David to be slain in battle. (One is inescapably reminded of a similar trick which later David played – successfully – on Uriah the Hittite [II Samuel] when he wanted Bath-Sheba, who was carrying their unborn child conceived in adultery, to be widowed and so made free to marry him.)

It may not seem to matter precisely which verse Rembrandt was illustrating, but I see his David as but a boy – the lad who had only shortly before faced and killed Goliath.[15] Also the muscles of Saul's hand look to me relaxed not tense on his spear, which is itself lying against his shoulder rather than held in a position from which it could be thrown at David without warning. The point of my reading of the painting, as distinct from Fowkes', is that I see David's 'harping' on the occasion depicted by Rembrandt as successful in dispelling the evil spirit while on the later occasions it signally failed to do so. Whether or not Saul's illness would be correctly diagnosed as schizophrenia, his violence appears not to have been assuaged by musical therapy after its initial success.

Unlike Fowkes, then, I believe Rembrandt shows Saul in the moment of balance when *violence becomes grief*, as if the sight of David and the magic of his hands on the harp restore to Saul his original feeling of great love for David; he is wiping away a tear with the curtain. If this be right, it is the interplay of Saul's relationship with David, and therefore, of course, with his own emotions engendered by David's role in his life, as Jonathan's soul-mate and as Saul's eventual successor as king, which determine the course of his illness. David's playing on the harp alone may not have been responsible for Saul's first recovery, and it subsequently failed to turn him from numerous attempts to kill David; on the contrary it seemed only to have exacerbated his mixed jealousy, hatred and fear of David, which his love for David and respect for his cunning – his head as well as his hands on his harp – could not overcome.

Some while ago I was watching a television documentary film on the therapeutic use of music to communicate and evoke new physical and psychologcal activity in mentally handicapped people of different ages. It was with awe and concern that I watched the musician-teacher-therapist achieving a degree of communication with each of the individual members of the class and, it seemed miraculously, evoking increasing degrees and a widening range of response. The task seemed to require almost angelic patience and the expectation that evidence of the opening of a channel of communication would appear, that there would be some feedback to justify any temptation to give up and to turn to some self-evidently more 'productive' work.

To call the task a 'labour of love' implies no underlying sentimentality.

I found myself identifying to an extent with the obvious aspirations of the teachers. But there was something else of which I was vaguely aware below the level of conscious formulation, and I sought to focus on it and clarify its implications. What impressed me at first was the realization that the members of the class were not only unaware of the nature of the experience they were being offered – the perception of rhythmic and musical notes and the recognition of their inter-relationships – but were even unaware that *anything* was being offered: their attention was elsewhere or they had not the motivation or the power to focus it – or perhaps they were absolutely and permanently incapable of giving attention to anything.

As the film progressed it became apparent that gradually and in a surprising number of instances, against *my* expectations, there were significant responses. Variations in vibrations if not of tones evoked clear evidence of appreciation, pleasure, joy, a *full* justification in human terms for all the time and effort expended. The pupils enjoyed what they did and what they heard, found they could make each a valid contribution to the music-making of a small band, accepted encouragement and would seek repetitions of the same involvement even if they could not apprehend the possibility of more complex sensual experience or of experimentation in listening and of performing.

Suddenly I realized the corresponding circumstances of which I was reminded – the supposition that teachers who are 'invisible' to us and to whom, therefore, we give no attention, may at certain times be signalling to us, it may be with the music of the spheres. They must be aware, as we are not, of the limitations of our level of waking consciousness. I visualize them as watching for and striving always to attract our erring attention. They seek to evoke that first response which would mean that some further communication is possible, some new range of experiences can be conveyed to develop us where, all along but beyond our ordinary powers to appreciate, a super-human potential slumbers within us. It is as if a new dimension awaits only our recognition of its existence and our wish to be shown how we may fruitfully engage with it. The late J. H. Reyner, who studied with Dr Maurice Nicoll for years longer than I did, wrote:[16]

One can evisage that the Universe may be populated by a large number of souls in different states of being, some in the process of descent from the Divine level of their creation, others at various stages of return – an idea portrayed in the well-known vision of the patriarch Jacob in which he saw a ladder set between heaven and earth on which were angels ascending and descending. One can surmise further that at every stage of the ascent an appropriate payment is required. Initially this is the effort to awaken the deeper levels of the mind but once this has been achieved a further and continuing payment is necessary. This appears to be of an increasingly impersonal quality which involves an obligation to help other souls on their respective journeys. Some may be required to maintain the constant supply of esoteric ideas on earth, represented in the medieval *Mutus Liber* as angels blowing trumpets in the ear of a sleeping figure. Others may be assigned to meet souls newly arrived in the bardo after the death of their physical body, or maybe to make contact in dreams with souls still in life.

Entirely fantasy? At most ninety-nine per cent.

---

[1] Michael Ratcliffe reviewing a production of the play by the Citizen's Theatre, Glasgow; *Observer*, 9 September 1984.

[2] A fascinating disquisition on the use of music in healing is to be found in *Through Music to the Self* by Peter Michael Hamel, op.cit.

[3] *Guardian*, 27 November 1979.

[4] *An Historical Account of the Heathen Gods and Heroes,* op.cit.

[5] *The Naked Face of Genius*, Gollancz, London, 1958.

[6] vol.I, page 229, *Berlioz and the Romantic Century*, Jaques Barzun, Gollancz, 1951.

[7] *Essays in Musical Analysis*, republished in *Some English Symphonists*, OUP, 1941.

[8] From sleeve-notes.

[9] And Op.25 No.11 was nicknamed 'Winter Winds', a title not sanctioned by the composer.

[10] WACC Journal, Vol.XXVI 2/1979.

[11] Foreword, p.viii, to *Rhythm, Music and Education* by Emile Jaques-Dalcroze, trans. Harold F. Rubinstein, Chatto & Windus, London, 1921.

[12] ibid. Foreword.

[13] An unnamed Indian sage, quoted in *Gurdjieff, Making a New World*, J. G. Bennett, Turnstone Books, London, 1973.

[14] Hamlyn, 1978.

[15] In *David, The Biography of a King* by Juan Bosch (trans. John Marks, Chatto

& Windus, 1966) these dramatic events are analysed and the biblical story of David's service with Saul and his subsequent reign is reviewed sympathetically but not sentimentally; the author rather convincingly discounts the attribution of Goliath's defeat to the boy David.

[16] *No Easy Immortality*, George Allen & Unwin, London, 1979. (Reyner explains that 'bardo' is the period of readjustment – symbolized as forty days – after the death of the body.)

MUSIC IN TWO MINDS: A POSTLUDE

Like countless, but carefully counted, bars rest for the triangle, months passed since I 'finished' writing the bulk of *Music to My Ear.* Years passed and this triangle player is, in effect, in another Movement.

Among the various momentous and mundane happenings in my life, which includes my immediate environment, I had since 1979 acquired and played – three times at least – a number of new records. My collection had swollen while my time for listening had shrunk. Many records, many albums (in this context many sets of records) would be played, henceforth, at most every two or three years. A regular and more frequent airing and hearing was no longer the point, if it ever had been. But a mystery remained niggling, unresolved, at the 'back of my mind' – what went on when I listened to my most-favourite-of-the-moment or most stimulating works on record while concentrating conscientiously on reading or writing? How could I be appreciating the complexities and subtleties of the music *and* doing justice at the same time to important thinking activities, where a lapse could have serious consequences? Yet that is what I seemed to be doing whenever I listened to music on record or radio at home.

An explanation did not seem to lie simply in the experience of a level of expanded consciousness induced by the practice of 'self-remembering' as I had studied it through the teaching of Gurdjieff, Ouspensky and Dr Nicoll. Awareness of oneself – of one's many selves

– and with it, a sharpened perception of the world, were not entirely irrelevant. The familiar experience which puzzled me involved attention, certainly but attention split between listening to music and my work. Self-remembering involves rather observation from front to back, a looking inwards, with objective self-observation (neither self-critical nor self-justifying), and at the same time outwards, from back to front, through attention given to received impressions.

Edward de Bono's idea of 'lateral thinking'[1] seemed also of possible relevance. But de Bono sought to encourage the use of a creative faculty of the mind, to encourage the exploration of alternatives to received ways of thinking about the world and about problems of all kinds. I did not find an explanation there for my working-cum-listening practice.

In the spring of 1983, however, there converged information from three separate sources which all seemed to point the same way. For some twenty years I had studied Sufism as taught and disseminated in his many books by Idries Shah. Associated with him in seminars and as an author whom Shah published, Robert Ornstein in his books *The Psychology of Consciousness** and *The Mind Field*** and Shah in his more recent works, notably *A Perfumed Scorpion* had introduced to me ideas about the independent functions of the left and right hemispheres of the brain. Then a book by a Californian art teacher, Betty Edwards, entitled *Drawing on the Right Side of the Brain*[2] encouraged me to find out for myself, through the practice of drawing, how differently the two hemispheres operate and to distinguish the 'feel' of their distinctive windows on the environment, here including the inner world, the environment of my thoughts and feelings. And, in the course of a year, from early in July 1982, I experienced, in the context of personal relations, the vivid, unconditioned, non-cerebral regard for other people which I realized characterized an activity of the right hemisphere, through my involvement with a learning system, Exegesis, from which I derived a number of experiential benefits.

That a knowledge of the functions of the two hemispheres, and a recognition of their value in ordinary life is not something only recently discovered in the West, may be inferred from a poem by Rudyard Kipling entitled *The Two-Sided Man*[3] from which Betty Edwards quotes:

Much I owe to the lands that grew–
More to the lives that fed –

But most to the Allah Who gave me Two
  Separate sides to my head

Much I reflect on the Good and the True
  In the faiths beneath the sun
But most upon Allah who gave me Two
  Sides to my head, not one.

I would go without shirt or shoe,
  Friend, tobacco or bread,
Sooner than lose for a minute the two
  Separate sides of my head!

In this highly charged panegyric, was Kipling, I wonder, inspired by a Sufi source?

The common usages of 'left' and 'right' delineate respectively the bad or awkward (sinister, gauche) and the good and acceptable (correct, praiseworthy). For the majority of people in our particular civilization left and right in these contexts refers to left-handedness and right-handedness. Physiologically the left side of the brain, the left hemisphere, governs the right side of the body and the right side, the right hemisphere, governs the left side of the body. Psychologically, even, it seems, for a number of left-handed people, the left hemisphere is responsible for verbalization, logical and analytical, rational and sequential thinking; the right hemisphere for intuition, insight and for holistic, spatial and simultaneous perceptiveness. These are two distinct ways of knowing the worlds of our senses and of ideas, two ways in which available information may be processed and experienced.

If unharmed by accident or disease, the two hemispheres are interconnected by a complex of nerve fibres (the *corpus callosum*) whose functions include the harmonization of the independent functioning of the hemispheres so as to convey a sense of single identity. With the resolution of conflicts which could, but for this harmonization, arise, goes the lack of ability to perceive the two different modes of activity and response to the same stimuli as it occurs during all periods of ordinary waking consciousness. In our society the dominance of the left hemisphere is promoted, almost exclusively, by our education system. Reason is allowed, indeed encouraged, especially in males, to prevail over a feeling response to almost every situation

175

encountered throughout our lives. An intuitive, non-logical approach or reaction is generally viewed with suspicion, denigrated, abhorred. We neglect or ignore the abundant evidence within ourselves of non-verbal communication and give it minimal attention and credibility.

With the aid of such exercises as Betty Edwards sets for drawing, in her book, and as so-called enlightenment cults provide by way of 'encounter' processes, it is possible to learn to know experientially, whenever attention is applied to the question, the difference between the dominance of one or other hemisphere.

As a child I was sometimes told that I was excessively argumentative. While arguing was one of *my* ways to gain attention, to be *right* and to control relationships, it was also a product of my conditioning. For me it was always important to promote battles of words and to win them: how else could I have survived all those hated nursery-governesses whose job it was to 'control' *me*? This left hemisphere activity is invaluable in a rational and materialistic world, essential for a successful legal practice and useful for social intercourse extending beyond trivialities and gossip. For me and for very many others with a similar environmental and educational background the appreciation of the non-verbal arts, notably music, painting and sculpture, was the subject of instantaneous conversion into rational and verbal terms by intellectual habit – by the taken-for-granted dominance of the left hemisphere, of which I was then ignorant, unconscious.

Evidently I failed to apply my efforts to know myself through self-observation with sufficient diligence to penetrate the obscurity of this profoundly 'dark' area of myself – dark, that is, *to* myself; people who were associated with me could see, but could not show me, that there was in me a barrier to my ability to feel empathy for others which bedevilled all those relationships in which I wished most strongly to find and to place the highest value, the greatest trust. That I had an underlying awareness of this unsatisfactory condition was apparent from a number of 'self-revealing' poems which I was agreeably impelled to compose after a heart-attack at the age of fifty-four, in 1975.

In the course of the 'initiation' Exegeis seminar, some seven years later, I saw, 'in a flash', the barrier's nature and its cause, both historically and psychologically. That was no rational, logical perception though it provided reason enough, and logicality. Over the following months relationships which mattered to me were transformed and consolidated. I had come to love my neighbours as I loved myself, through the grace of instant inner reconciliation.

Associated with this newly found experience of joy and energy was a feeling of a 'release-of-love' not confined to those closest to me in kinship or friendship, or to any particular category of persons. The feeling is not sentimental nor is it, in a conventional sense, religious; but it subsists essentially in 'one world' where the interdependence and yet relative independence of all human beings, indeed all creatures, all nature within the biosphere, is self-evident, perfect and *right* – a manifestation of the right side of the brain.

Gradually, I learned to use a number of faculties which were formerly only of theoretical significance for me. Among them was the practice of looking steadily at a person (not the same as staring) until preconceptions and inferences derived from conditioning based on appearances, seem to wither away, cease to monopolize my attention. Then, even without, though preferably with shared eye contact, through the appropriate functioning of the right cerebral hemisphere, I am free to perceive 'what is so' about the person I am regarding. There is a directness, a cleanliness, a purity of self-will in this experience which betokens its validity; and it is no less applicable to things than to people.[4]

Betty Edwards' book focused this looking – looking without attitudes towards or against, or emotional identification with anything about the object observed – on the development of an ability to draw. Hitherto I was handicapped in relation to this ability, as are very many others, by the dominance of the left side of the brain. I allowed that side, however, to notice and to comment on her book, where it digressed from advocacy of the practice of right-side-of-brain perception and drawing. From Betty Edwards' final list of comparative ways of knowing, I was particularly interested to note – '*successive*' from the left and '*simultaneous*' from the right hemisphere. Which precisely brings me to confront again my search for an understanding of the ways I am affected by the impact and influences of music.

It is tempting to claim that my appreciation of music while I am engaged in cerebral work is 'obviously' with the right side of my brain. 'Obviously', however, obviously represents only a typical conclusion of the left side. It is useless (agrees the left side) to rely on left side perception, deduction, logic or analysis to determine a reality about the functioning of the right side. There may be no reason to assume that the left side has 'got it wrong' but there is no good reason to assume that it has 'got it completely right'. For those who can recognize the effects of the left side's dominance it is imperative, mandatory, to consult the right hemisphere for a true answer to the question as to what is being experienced through the right hemisphere.

The right hemisphere is not given to verbalization. It brushes aside such a question, being concerned with the experience of 'what is so', not with a secondhand interpretation, an inevitably incomplete verbal rationalization, just as words are generally accepted as inadequate to define the flavour of a strawberry. When a verbal formula is used to describe the experience, truth – the truth, the whole truth and nothing but the truth – is not in it. No wonder that a book devoted to the search for an explanation as to why I choose, given the opportunity, to listen to one piece of music or one performance on record rather than another, is meaningful on several different levels. I choose what to listen to next by inclinations motivated too subtly for verbal description. Sometimes choices have been apparently spontaneous while others, for which a logical reason or series of reasons could be given, were made deliberately.

One evening, my wife, Joy, and I had the company of a couple of acquaintances who turned out to be less than fascinating for us. At the restaurant where we all met, the food was adequate but not 'great'. The ambience was, for me, grotesquely disagreeable: we were assailed by loud canned music consisting of bloody snippets – they were too short for bleeding chunks – of popular classics. I didn't time them but would guess the average length was two minutes and, without a break, this 'selection' out-poured for some three hours. It rendered difficult conversation no easier, failed to oil the cogs of possible conviviality and had me answering an innocent question about my views on a particular model of the Jaguar car with 'this bit? It's the Hallelujah Chorus from *Messiah*, [modestly] I think' – information of no conceivable interest to my opposite number for whom music of what he called 'considerable emotional significance', was limited absolutely to the violin concertos of Mendelssohn, Bruch (No.1, no doubt) and Tchaikovsky.

By courtesy of my left hemisphere, I can say that when the left side of the brain is dominant the right may be dormant or simply differently active. Having experienced the immediacy of perception with the right side when able to look with appropriate objectivity at a person, a picture or any other object, I ponder (with the left side) about right hemisphere perception of a piece of music, the right hemisphere not being accustomed to sequential appreciation. For the right hemisphere, in practice never mind theory, that can present no problem, however. A musical work is indeed 'all of a piece'. Its essential extension in time which, for the left hemisphere is sequential, will be appreciated as a whole, as 'what is so', by the right hemisphere.

There is a temptation here to duck an issue. What does the right side of the brain know of wrong notes? Or of dynamics or emphasis 'unacceptable' in the sense of being contrary to expectation based on conditioning which is responsible for left-side reaction? *I* am aware immediately of the experience of an unsatisfactory performance, or momentary lapse, when listening to a familiar work on the radio while doing my cerebral, word-orientated work: where is *that* 'I' conscious? On this problem I reflect. I do not seek to worry out an answer by constructing a logical edifice, such as 'since I am not taking in the music with the left, word-and-sequence-orientated side of my brain, it must be the case that . . .' something or other. I am presented with the feeling, derived from non-verbal experience, in a flash, that the right side of the brain 'knows'; it hears 'what is so' when it hears the wrong note, and so on; and it relates to that with its own memory of 'what is so' when the right note is played. An association to be valid, to be recognized, does not have to be verbal; or sequential. Nor does it have to be non-verbal or isolated in time in order to register in the right hemisphere.

There is an awareness that a part of me is listening to music evidenced by my immediate reaction if there is a breakdown in transmission or reproduction before a work's proper end. This awareness extends to wrong notes and other subjectively assessed imperfections; but also to passages which give me especial pleasure. Meanwhile, my more conscious, right hemisphere appreciation weaves in and out.[5]

With music we are concerned with non-verbal communication, save when words are set to it. Deryck Cooke's *The Language of Music*, a characteristic left hemisphere analysis of right hemisphere experience, is, like the languages of gesture or posture or facial expression, a substitute for communication by speech. A single note struck, blown, plucked or drawn, though not strictly instantaneous (the reverberations from one striking of a gong or bell may continue audibly for several seconds) does not of itself constitute 'music', unless that word is used in relation to music sculptures. An essential characteristic of composed, as distinct from some improvised, music is the 'sense' conveyed by its having a beginning and an end, with sounds between which lead, meaningfully not randomly from the one to the other: like, in this respect, a verbalized story. The length of what goes on between the start and the finish decides how long, in time, the listener to music must wait for the completion of the non-verbal journey.

For the unadventurous a short journey, perhaps frequently undertaken, is satisfying if the return, by the final cadence, is, comfortably, to 'home'. That is all very well, but for a little while only. For some people such a limited exercise not only fails to satisfy; it is soon found boring and may come to act like an aural prison yard to which the reaction may be as strong as a full-throated scream, though this is generally suppressed to inaudibility or mild protest.

The adventurous are prepared to be kept waiting, between the first notes and the last, provided the passage of music in the middle is interesting enough to hold attention or to stimulate agreeable day-dreaming.

If that were all there were to it, why listen to any piece of music more than once? Because (my left side acknowledges) I may wish to enjoy, directly or perversely, the same reactions as on the first hearing or different ones according to mood, association or company; or to recognize and be reminded that once is not enough, even for a work duly heard conscientiously from beginning to end; and indeed to recognize that not only is once not enough, but that to listen to any finite number of works, heard once or any greater number of times, is not enough. Through such repetition *there is no escape* from a hell of inevitable, complete and eternal predictability; I am reminded of the hell depicted in Jean-Paul Sartre's play *Huis Clos*.[6] And between the functioning of left and right hemispheres there needs to be and there is (I feel intuitively) a possibility of 'escape'.

That music can remind me of such a possibility I know from my emotional response to the open-ended *Last Post*. I do not believe that the emotion was – is – derived from conditioning or from association, for example with the ceremony at the Cenotaph on Armistice Day, since I have never attended a burial or memorial service at which the

Last Post was sounded. Indeed my chief memory of its impact on me comes from that army course in Uxbridge in 1940, as I lay on my bed ready for sleep.

That I do not choose what I will hear from the functioning of either the left or right hemisphere of my brain, should be self-evident even from my inevitably partial analysis in this book. On every occasion when I come to make a choice my decision, mixed conscious and unconscious, is compounded of numerous elements, which in turn affect the balance of decision-making between the two hemispheres. An understanding of the essential interaction of the frontal lobes with the activities of the hemispheres, to plan and to make any decision, I derived from *The Sphinx and the Rainbow*[7] where Dr David Loye surveys the disciplines of neurophysiology, psychology, parapsychology and theoretical physics. He describes notably how the frontal brain may interact with the right and left hemispheres in forecasting the future and suggests how planning is a function of the faculty of prediction – accessible, to a greater or lesser degree, to everyone. The brain, in planning how best to satisfy a desire, exercises the capacity to predict the likely result of the implementation of any one of the alternative possibilities.

Dr Loye refers[8] to J. W. Dunne's theory of serial time and to J. B. Priestley's *Man and Time* but seems to have misread the writings of both. He gives the impression that he knows of Ouspensky's 'three time view' as he calls it, only from Priestley's summary. In Ouspensky's chapter entitled 'A New Model of the Universe',[9] a universe is postulated which is limited to six dimensions – the three dimensions of space and one each of time, eternity and all possibilities, at right angles, as it were, to all the other dimensions in which 'all possible futures really happen'[10] – and all possible pasts too co-exist eternally. According to this theory of Ouspensky there could be no additional dimensions since any reality not extant in the sixth dimension would, by definition, be *im*possible. Ouspensky's eternally existent sixth dimension is precisely where free-will may operate in a complete system, unlimited save for the literally impossible.

For my purposes other most significant insights, to which Loye refers, are those developed by Professor David Bohm who had many discussions with Einstein and an extensive correspondence with him from 1951 to 1956, though he was not, as Loye suggests, associated with

Einstein in his unsuccessful efforts to produce the unified field theory. Later Bohm and Karl Pribram independently experimented with, and then discussed their ideas about, holography – the use of laser beams, with mirrors, photographic plates and objects, to project, store and distribute three-dimensional images. Bohm found the hologram an instrument whose properties might be analogous to certain features of the universe itself to explain, upon its theoretical extension in motion as the holomovement, such mysteries as images in the human mind, the representation of images in telepathic communication and precognition, the existence, storage and retrieval of memories and the limitations of human consciousness.[11]

According to Loye (with his emphasis), the hologram showed Bohm 'how seemingly separate objects could in fact be connected together in the underlying, interpenetrating way that physics already indicated was operating in the Universe . . . He decided to call the underlying, outlying, or higher unseen reality the *implicate order*. This was the place for containing all that was latent or *nonmanifest*. In contrast to it was this present, here-and-now, seen and heard and felt reality we are all familiar with and move among: the *explicate order*. This was the place for all that was manifest . . . He perceived that out of the implicate order all things *unfolded* into our sensate reality, and out of this explicate order that we see, hear, and feel, all things are then *enfolded* back into the underlying, outlying, or higher hidden reality.'

Bohm[12] attributes to Pribram the suggestion derived from the latter's work on brain structure, that 'memories are generally recorded all over the brain in such a way that information concerning a given object or reality is not stored in a particular cell or localized part of the brain but rather that all the information is enfolded over the whole. This storage resembles a hologram in its function, but its actual structure is much more complex. We can then suggest that when the "holographic" record in the brain is suitably activated, the response is to create a pattern of nervous energy constituting a partial experience similar to that which produced the "hologram" in the first place.' But it is also significantly different in three respects – it is less detailed, memories from many different times may merge together, and memories may be connected by association and by logical thought to give a certain further order to the whole pattern. And further, 'if sensory data is also being attended to at the same time, the whole of this response from memory will, in general, fuse with the nervous

182

excitation coming from the senses to give rise to an overall experience in which memory, logic, and sensory activity combine into a singly unanalyseable whole'.

Bohm acknowledges that consciousness involves, in addition, at least also awareness, attention, perception and acts of understanding, going beyond a mechanistic response. In studying such factors contributing to the whole of a reaction from memory, Bohm suggests that 'we may be coming closer to the essence of actual conscious experience than is possible merely by discussing patterns of excitation of the sensory nerves and how they may be recorded in memory'.

He goes on to commend reflection on what happens in certain experiences which can provide valuable clues about such subtle faculties.

Consider, for example, what takes place when one is listening to music. At a given moment a certain note is being played but a number of the previous notes are still 'reverberating' in consciousness. Close attention will show that it is the simultaneous presence and activity of all these reverberations that is responsible for the direct and immediately felt sense of movement, flow and continuity. To hear a set of notes so far apart in time that there is no such reverberation will destroy altogether the sense of a whole unbroken, living movement that gives meaning and force to what is heard.

It is clear from the above that one does not experience the actuality of this whole movement by 'holding on' to the past, with the aid of a memory of the sequence of notes, and comparing this past with the present. Rather, as one can discover by further attention, the 'reverberations' that make such an experience possible are not memories but are rather active transformations of what came earlier, in which are to be found not only a generally diffused sense of the original sounds, with an intensity that falls off, according to the time elapsed since they were picked up by the ear, but also various emotional responses, bodily sensations, incipient muscular movements, and the evocation of a wide range of yet further meanings, often of great subtlety. One can thus obtain a direct sense of how a sequence of notes is enfolding into many levels of consciousness, and of how at any given moment, the transformation flowing out of many such enfolded notes interpenetrate and intermingle to give rise to an immediate and primary feeling of movement.

Bohm draws attention to the 'striking parallel' of this activity in consciousness to the activity which he has proposed for what he calls 'the implicate order in general', by reference to a model of an electron described earlier in his book. In the enfoldment, in various degrees, of 'a co-present set of different transformed ensembles which inter-penetrate and intermingle . . . there is a radical change, not only of form but also of structure, in the entire set of ensembles [a "meta-morphosis"]; and yet a certain totality of order in the ensembles remains invariant, in the sense that in all these changes a subtle but fundamental similarity of order is preserved'. (Of course he is here using the word 'ensembles' in a general not a musical sense.)

Bohm concludes these reflections on music in relation to his theme (his emphasis throughout):

In the music, there is, as we have seen, a basically similar transformation (of notes) in which a certain order can also be seen to be preserved. The key difference in these two cases [the electron and the music] is that for our model of the electron an enfolded order is grasped *in thought*, as the presence together of many different but interrelated degrees of transformation of ensembles, while for the music, it is *sensed immediately* as the presence together of many different but interrelated degrees of transformations of tones and sounds. In the latter, there is a feeling of both tension and harmony between the various co-present transformations, and this feeling is indeed what is primary in the apprehension of the music in its undivided state of flowing movement.

In listening to music, *one is therefore directly perceiving an implicate order*. Evidently this order is *active* in the sense that it continually flows into emotional, physical, and other responses, that are inseparable from the transformations out of which it is essentially constituted.

As I understood the import of David Bohm's thesis in the passages I have quoted I found it extraordinarily satisfying as soon as I encountered it. Only as I pondered its implications for my own quest in this book did I begin to perceive its relevance to two other ideas which had hovered around my ruminations.

The first of these ideas is the matter of the energy conveyed by music – the different energies conveyed by different music.[13] When I take in any energy-giving substance it is digested, that is transmuted, and stored or discharged as energy, according to its nature and quality and the characteristics of my receptive organism. I take in energy in varied forms – an expected or an unexpected blow, food, liquid refreshment both non-alcoholic and alcoholic, the air I breathe and all kinds of impressions which my total being is equipped to respond or react to or to absorb and digest.[14] Music enters me as, primarily, an aural impression. When transmuted into energy this may be discharged through the stimulation it provides to cause physical or emotional reaction. Very loud music, especially with a strong, regular beat will stimulate a very powerful physical and emotional response, hence the popularity with young people of pop concerts and discos.

A materially identical item of ordinary food or drink may affect me differently on different occasons; that is not surprising when the receptive body – mine in this instance – is changed by such factors as relative hunger or satiation, tiredness or freshness, general or specific illness or health, and emotional states of upset or wellbeing. These factors dictate the effective digestion of the solid or liquid intake and so the destination of the various energies made available with every mouthful or gulp. Similar factors self-evidently operate in the same way with all intakes of impressions. That the factors are many, complex and subtle is only to be expected hence they may defy any attempt at analysis. But that does not invalidate the proposition; indeed it may be taken to reinforce it.

The other idea which I have touched on earlier, is one which I have come to regard as of supreme significance to an understanding of the place of music in human life both historically and, at every instant, contemporaneously. It is the recognition of the essential connectedness of all human beings, alive or dead; indeed the idea is necessarily to be extended then to every animate being and inanimate object existing in the universe.[15]

To draw together these strands of ideas I would emphasize that their significance for anyone depends upon a prior acceptance of the idea that only a tiny proportion of the world we inhabit is available to our perception through our senses: that our coming into the experience we have of life, of which we are aware through the state we call ordinary consciousness, is represented to us through a minuscule range of the total of vibrations known so far to science, so that there must be a vastly greater range inaccessible to our senses and normal waking consciousness. This is to emphasize, at its simplest, the distinction between Bohm's explicate and implicate orders.

Underlying the various responses to music of people with the widest variety of taste or interest in it, there is, I feel, a subconscious realization that people are somehow connected through music even within the explicate order. When I raise my fiddle to my chin, tune it and hold my bow poised above the strings by the bridge it matters not what I intend to play or the standards of my musicality or technique. I am automatically and inevitably connected with generations of violin makers, composers for and performers on the violin; and so with the violin's forebears and instruments akin to the violin on which is played the music of our and of other cultures; and with all those other instruments for which music has been composed to be performed with violins; and so with the composers and performers of music for any of those other instruments without violins; and with everyone in every audience who has ever heard a performance of music composed with or without a violin alone or in combination with any of those other instruments . . .

Over the centuries that vision connects millions of people through music. Moreover it connects together everyone living today who has ever heard music performed or made a musical noise through the influence of environment or conditioning; it may seem to exclude people who are tone deaf and those who are completely without the sense of hearing, but they will be no less connected through rhythmic vibrations and through the impact, however slight of any of the visual or verbal arts or, almost for sure, even through the culinary art!

The starving are no less connected with the well-fed than with each other, that is, the 'haves' with the 'have-nots'; women with men, homo- with hetero-sexuals; the mobile with the immobile; terrorists and torturers with their victims; the pious with the blasphemous; 'them' with 'us'; the listeners to the same or different radio programmes, like the viewers of television, all the readers of newspapers, periodicals and books and the illiterate who can nevertheless speak and understand speech; and those who prefer Mozart to Bach with those others who prefer Bach.

There is no living person who is not in innumerable and definable ways connected with every other person, living or dead. This is a fact of life which we ignore so as to maintain an artificial distinction, an irrelevant sense of superiority or inferiority. Sadly it may often be convenient for us to behave as if we are not like others and that they are not – as they truly are – as close to us as brothers and sisters. Indeed, I am not 'my brother's keeper': I *am* my brother – in Bohm's implicate order which (if his theory be right) underlies and interpenetrates the whole of the manifest universe we inhabit. And the whole universe, manifest and (to us) non-manifest – embracing both the explicate and the implicate orders – is more magnificent and more complex than we can conceive or are ever likely to realize to even a tiny extent in the course of a lifetime.

It is no wonder, then, that if we are touched or affected or moved by any music at all, in any circumstances, we may find its influence mysterious. Its significance derives from the implicate order of which we are barely, if at all or if ever, aware. Yet without Bohm's implicate order – or something like it – the explicate order, the world as we know it (or think we know it), through manifestations open to our organs of perception, could not exist; and anyway would be incapable of rational or scientific explanation. Music is one of the supreme art-forms reminding us subliminally of the unmanifest inter-connectedness of everything in the universe.

Hark! The herald angels sing . . .

---

[1] *Lateral Thinking*, Ward Lock Educational, London, 1970. *Op.cit. **ibid. 1983. Octagon Press, London, 1978 (e.g. p.30 '. . . Sufi education aims at getting both sides of the brain to work, and helping them to operate at times in concert, and not alternately'.)

[2] Souvenir Press Ltd, 1981; Fontana Paperbacks 1982 in the UK.

[3] *Rudyard Kipling's Verse*, Hodder & Stoughton, London, 1927.

[4] Jean Genet in an essay entitled *Something Which Seemed to Resemble Decay* (translated from the French by Bernard Frechtman), describes a similar experience which led him to observe 'No man was my brother: every man was myself, but temporarily isolated in his individual shell . . . I felt no tenderness, no affection for that self which was outside my individual appearance.' The experience caused Genet infinite sadness, 'in a kind of state of self-disgust' – loving his neighbour as himself, precisely. (cf. 'Anteus', No.54, Spring 1985; p.108ff.)

[5] This section is based on my own experience of the functions of the left and right hemispheres in relation to music: the existence of scientific confirmation as I subsequently found, is outlined and quoted in Chapter 6, 'Musical

Intelligence' of *Frames of Mind* by Howard Gardner, Basic Books Inc., New York, 1983.

[6] trans. Stuart Gilbert, Hamish Hamilton, 1946.

[7] Dr David Loye, Shambhala Publications, Boulder & London, 1983.

[8] ibid. Chapter 14, and Notes to Chapter 5 and Chapter 14.

[9] In the book of that title first published in 1931 by Kegan Paul, Trench, Trubner & Co. Ltd.

[10] Quoted by Loye from a doctoral thesis by Hugh Everett III in *The Many-Worlds Interpretation of Quantum Mechanics*, co-authors De Witt & Graham, 1973.

[11] See Bohm's *Wholeness and the Implicate Order*, Routledge & Kegan Paul, London, 1980, pp. 172–207.

[12] ibid. p.198 et seq.

[13] 'The essential ingredient for any successful rock group is energy – the ability to give out energy, to receive energy from the audience, and to give it back to the audience. A rock concert is in fact a rite involving the evocation and transmutation of energy. Rock stars may be compared to priests . . . The Led Zeppelin show depends heavily on volume, repetition and drums. It bears some resemblance to the trance music found in Morocco, which is magical in origin and purpose – that is, concerned with the evocation and control of spiritual forces. In Morocco, musicians are also magicians. Gnaoua music is used to drive out evil spirits. The music of Jajouka evokes the God Pan, Pan God of Panic, representing the real magical forces that sweep away the spurious. It has to be remembered that the origin of all the arts – music, painting and writing – is magical and evocative; and that magic is always used to obtain some magical result. In the Led Zeppelin concert, the result aimed at would seem to be the creation of energy in the performers and the audience. For such magic to succeed, it must tap the sources of magical energy, and this can be dangerous.' William S. Burroughs on Led Zeppelin from *Rock Magic* (*Crawdaddy*, June 1975).

[14] A recognition of impressions as a 'food' vitally important for life is fundamental to the system of ideas taught by Gurdjieff and Ouspensky.

[15] See the chapter 'Experimental Mysticism' in Ouspensky's *A New Model of the Universe*, op.cit., especially p.326.

BIBLIOGRAPHY

Deryck Cooke *The Language of Music* OUP, 1959
Donald Tovey *Beethoven* OUP, 1944
Fritjof Capra *The Tao of Physics* Fontana, 1976
Peter Michael Hamel (trans. Peter Lemesurier) *Through Music to the Self* Compton Press, 1978
William King *Heathen Gods and Heroes* Centaur Press, 1965
Curt Sachs *The Wellsprings of Music* Da Capo Press, NY, 1962
Robert Graves *The Greek Myths* Penguin Books, 1955
Jean Charon *The Unknown Spirit* Coventure 1983
G. I Gurdjieff *All and Everything* RKP, 1950
Fania Fenelon *The Musicians of Auschwitz* Michael Joseph, 1977
Anthony Hopkins *Understanding Music* Dent, 1979
Sir Yehudi Menuhin *Unfinished Journey* Macdonald and Jane's, 1977
Christopher Wright *Rembrandt: Self-Portraits* Gordon Fraser, 1982
Robert Ornstein *The Psychology of Consciousness* W. H. Freeman, San Francisco, 1972
Dr Maurice Nicoll *Psychological Commentaries on the Teachings of Gurdjieff and Ouspensky* Vincent Stuart, 1952
Agatha Fassett *The Naked Face of Genius* Gollancz, 1958
Jaques Barzin *Berlioz and the Romantic Century* Gollancz, 1951
Donald Tovey *Some English Symphonists* OUP, 1941
Christopher Fowkes *The Life of Rembrandt* Hamlyn, 1978

J. H. Reyner *No Easy Immortality* George Allen & Unwin, 1979
Edward de Bono *Lateral Thinking* Ward Lock Educational, 1970
Robert Ornstein *The Mind Field* Octagon Press, 1983
Idries Shah *The Perfumed Scorpion* Octagon Press, 1978
Betty Edwards *Drawing on the Right Side of the Brain* Fontana Paperbacks, 1982
David Bohm *Wholeness and the Implicate Order* RKP, 1980
P. D. Ouspensky *A New Model of the Universe* Kegan Paul, 1931

INDEX